"Christ called His followers to be b[...] all to stand for truth, to love people [...] promised to reward us richly when we do. In this book Ken Harrison details promises Jesus made to us when we live out our faith in courage despite the cowardly world we live in. Ken's unique background gives him powerful stories that bring the truth to life in a way that is completely engrossing. Few followers of Christ are aware of all the promises He has made to reward those who give all to follow Him. Ken does a great job of encouraging God's children to give all so that they can receive everything that their Father has promised."

TONY EVANS, PASTOR, SPEAKER, AUTHOR, AND RADIO AND TELEVISION BROADCASTER

"Ken Harrison is truly a 'brother in the struggle,' speaking truth to power. God isn't looking for perfect people, He's looking for people with the obedience and faith to occupy God's kingdom on earth. Ken's must-read book challenges us to be the people God has called us to be."

DR. ALVEDA KING, GUARDIAN OF THE KING FAMILY LEGACY

"Ken Harrison is not only a close friend; he's a man of God leading men of God. Through *A Daring Faith in a Cowardly World*, Ken shares a message applicable to all followers of Christ—we are meant for more. More faith. More courage. More freedom. Take Ken's words to heart and watch your life burst with the power of resurrection."

SAM RODRIGUEZ, PRESIDENT OF NHCLC, PASTOR, AUTHOR OF *PERSEVERE WITH POWER*, AND EXECUTIVE PRODUCER

A
DARING
FAITH
IN A
COWARDLY
WORLD

A DARING FAITH IN A COWARDLY WORLD

Live a Life Without Waste, Regret, or Anything Unfinished

KEN HARRISON

W PUBLISHING GROUP

AN IMPRINT OF THOMAS NELSON

A Daring Faith in a Cowardly World

Published in Nashville, Tennessee, by W Publishing, an imprint of Thomas Nelson.

Thomas Nelson titles may be purchased in bulk for educational, business, fundraising, or sales promotional use. For information, please email SpecialMarkets@ThomasNelson.com.

ISBN 978-0-7852-9079-7 (audiobook)
ISBN 978-0-7852-9078-0 (eBook)
ISBN 978-0-7852-9077-3 (TP)

Library of Congress Cataloging-in-Publication Data

Library of Congress Control Number: 2022931194

Printed in the United States of America

22 23 24 25 26 LSC 10 9 8 7 6 5 4 3 2 1

To Norton Rainey—Sr. Norton has been an unceasing teacher about crowns and rewards for many decades and I count it as a privilege to have been discipled by such a great man. Norton and I covered many miles together teaching and discipling people from all walks of life before Norton succumbed to advanced Alzheimer's disease. Norton will receive a rich reward in heaven for his relentless dedication to teaching his fellow believers the advanced truths about Christ.

CONTENTS

CONTENTS

FOREWORD

KEN HARRISON CARRIES THE SUPERNATURAL ANOINTING OF God to help every man become who God created him to be. As followers of Jesus Christ, we must engage in the "good works" that the apostle Paul said we were created to do (Eph. 2:10). How do we do it?

Through practical steps, scriptural truth, and fascinating stories from his unique personal experiences, Ken shows us not only *why* we must become the men God desires, but *how* we can accomplish it.

When we first met, at the urging of three-time Dallas Cowboys Super Bowl champion Chad Hennings, we discussed how important it is for all believers to grasp the truth of God's kingdom will being done on earth as it is in heaven. "The earth is the Lord's." Yes, Planet earth. And He left us as His family to be wise overseers. Early in the conversation with Ken, I said forcefully, "God is building one kingdom—His. We must all decide if we are going to join Him, building His kingdom by gathering or scattering."

Ken was captivated by that thought, but more importantly, it was obvious he had been captured by our heavenly Father's heart. God had clearly led Ken to believe that God's will could be done on earth and that He has designed men to lead by inspiring all believers to find meaningful, fulfilling life by losing theirs to fulfill God's kingdom purpose.

In this truly inspiring, motivating book he shows men the importance of loving their wives as Christ loves the church and training their children to know and do God's will because it's the greatest source of joy and meaningful life. He believes that as earthly fathers we can give our families clear glimpses of the heavenly Father. We can impact our neighbors by sharing God's transforming truth with unconditional love and genuine compassion.

Ken challenges all men to live with such honor and integrity that everyone notices an undeniable difference in our lives. He does not use legalistic coercion, but biblical inspiration, holding to the promise that our commitment to fulfill God's kingdom purpose is amazingly meaningful.

Finally, he makes it very clear we must learn to lead, beginning in the home; then the church, the community, and the nation. To do so is not only the fulfillment of God's calling on our lives, but a privilege and a thrill when done in obedience to our heavenly Father.

I greatly appreciate and encourage everyone who, like Ken Harrison, is seeking to know God's will and desires to put it into action by applying the truths found in this book. As you read through these pages, I believe God will inspire you to fulfill His dreams for and through your life. You will discover, as Ken and I have found, the unspeakable joy and excitement available in Christ by pursuing God's kingdom purpose fulfilled on earth—right here, right now! It can be done, and the wisdom in this book will help inspire men to lead.

James Robison
Founder and President
LIFE Outreach International

PREFACE

WHAT'S THE POINT OF IT ALL?

I OFTEN WONDERED WHAT THE POINT WAS. THE POINT OF dying to self, giving to the poor, standing for justice—even when it cost me. I'd been raised in the church with some good Bible teaching, but my understanding of the Christian life was severely lacking. What I understood was that Jesus sacrificed it all on the cross to save us from our sins, and we had nothing to do with it. This is true, but the teaching also seemed to imply that there was nothing to do after our salvation. I was told that our righteousness was like filthy rags—also true. Yet Jesus makes all kinds of demands of us after we're saved. If He did it all on the cross and our righteousness is like filthy rags, why does He make demands of us that seem impossible?

At the age of twelve, I started diligently reading the Bible to find the answers my teachers couldn't give. Why did Jesus tell Nicodemus all he needed to do to be saved was believe, but He told the rich young ruler to give away all his money if he wanted to inherit eternal life? Why does Jesus say that whoever believes in Him will "not perish" (John 3:16) but then says, "Those of you who do not give up everything you have cannot be my disciples" (Luke 14:33 NIV)? Why did Paul say in Romans 2 that God will repay each person for what he or she has done, that those who have persisted in doing good works will receive eternal life, but then spent the next several chapters explaining that salvation has nothing to do with works?

What's the point of the Christian life? If we're all going to the same place in heaven or the same place in hell, why did Paul go through so much misery to spread the gospel? He was beaten, tortured, stoned, imprisoned multiple times, often hungry and cold . . . Why did he go through so much if he was only going to receive the same as the person who did nothing? If the worldly Christian who lived only for himself ends up with the same eternity as those who were burned alive for the gospel, why would people like Hudson Taylor, Mother Teresa, Thomas Aquinas, and Martin Luther all suffer great misery to spread the good news of Jesus? How does that line up with the statements of Jesus about giving up all?

The fact is we have the chance to reign with God forever, to be coheirs with Jesus Christ, and to have close communion with our loving Father both in this life and the next. That depends on what we do after we're saved. Good works have no value for our salvation because we're dead in our sins. We can be saved only by God's grace through faith, and even the faith we exercise is a gift from Him. But the moment we're saved and filled with His Spirit, we're alive, and then what we do matters greatly.

This book is designed to be an encouragement to you to stay the course, persevere through the trials, and patiently wait on the Lord, for the reward is great to all who are passionate for the things of God. It's hard. Father knows it, and He is there to help us along the way. Let's dig in to how we grow in holiness so that we can experience the fullness of everything God gave us the day He walked out of that grave.

PART 1

CALLED TO A DARING FAITH

WHAT WILL WE TELL JESUS WE DID WITH OUR LIVES?

For we must all appear before the judgment seat of Christ, so that each of us may receive what is due us for the things done while in the body, whether good or bad.

2 CORINTHIANS 5:10 NIV

Too many Christians are more concerned with God's kingdom to come than they are about the one that's here right now. Why are we so concerned about what Satan is going to do in the end times? We should be thinking about what God's going to do—through us! If we would just lose ourselves in His kingdom purposes, we could change the world!

JAMES ROBISON[1]

IN 1997 I GOT HIT BY A WAVERUNNER. THE IMPACT THREW me several yards from the jet ski I was on, breaking most of the ribs on my right side and rupturing some organs. Through the fog in my brain, I was still able to process that if I passed out in the water, even with a life vest on, I'd drown. Somehow I climbed around the lip of the jet ski and waited to pass out.

When my friends got me to the emergency room, I told the nurse, "I've been hit by a WaveRunner! I'm bleeding internally, and I might be dying." She didn't take me seriously, ordering me to sit down and fill out forms. I watched people with bumps and bruises called in before me as I started to feel dizzy from loss of blood. After a while I walked back up and said, "I'm bleeding internally and might be dying." She rewarded me with more forms.

After a half hour or so, I was led back to a doctor, who felt around my ribs, asking what happened. As I told him and winced in pain, he screamed, "This man is bleeding internally! He's dying on my table!"

"This is what I've been telling you people," I said. I might have been about to die, but I wasn't going to let the opportunity for a good "Told you so!" pass.

They ushered me in for a CAT scan, accidentally dropping me from one gurney to another, causing me to pass out from the pain. When I came to, the young doctor, who had the bedside manner of George Patton, said, "Look, dude, here's the deal. You ruptured your liver. We're going to take a look at this scan. If you damaged less than forty percent, we'll life flight you to a trauma hospital and cut it out, but it'll grow back. If you ruptured more than forty percent, you've got about five hours until you're dead."

"How will I die?" I asked.

"What do you mean?" he asked. "You won't have a liver."

"Yeah, but what kills me? What will I feel?"

"Oh," he said, "your body will poison itself." He walked out and I didn't see him for an hour.

It was quite an hour, lying on the gurney, wondering if I felt my body poisoning itself, unable to filter out the toxins. Mostly, though, a thought struck me deep and hard. What would I say to Jesus when I was standing in front of Him? Wondering that in theory is one thing; wondering it when it may be four hours away is another.

It was a strange experience because I'd faced death so often as a Los Angeles police officer but always in a flood of adrenaline. It had been gunfire, screaming, bravado, blood. Afterward, we'd all gather around and recount the story and laugh at one another. Facing death lying in a hospital bed as pain pierced the shock was different. It was a time of deep introspection, and my thoughts centered on being judged by Christ. There was no bravado. No one was gathering around in a couple of hours to recount the story and nominate anyone for an award. I'd been hit by a WaveRunner and might soon be dead. That was it. The gift of life might soon be over. What had I done with that gift?

The verse that starts this chapter says we'll stand before the judgment seat of Christ. This judgment seat of Christ was not part of my biblical education. I don't recall ever being taught about it. In fact, "works don't matter" had been pounded into my head. I'd been taught that one's works were only proof of being saved, but they didn't matter. Everything one did was filthy rags, so why try?

Interestingly, though, I had been a boy and young man of Scripture. I had disciplined myself to read three chapters of the Bible every day since the age of twelve. I knew the Bible extremely well. Since I know the Bible, when the matter of death and eternity was staring me in the face, my thoughts weren't on doctrine; they were on what I'd read in Scripture. Romans 2:6 kept pounding through my head: "He will repay each one according to his works." I knew then and there that my works did matter. Not for salvation, which is by grace alone, but for the status and place in eternity.

As I faced what might be impending death, the only thought on my mind was this: *When Jesus asks what I did with what He gave me, what will I say?* I was thirty years old and had no answer. I was a good guy. I never cheated on my wife. I was a police officer. That rang hollow. I'd been immersed in the Bible since the age of twelve, had gone to Christian schools and colleges— but what difference had my time on earth made? Who had been blessed? Who'd been fed? Who would point at me and say that their life had been changed because of me? No one.

The young doctor walked in with a grin. "Good news, dude. You ruptured your kidney and only lacerated your liver, so you're cool."

"That's good news?" I asked.

"Well, yeah, you've got two kidneys, sooo . . . And your lung is ruptured, too, and you broke a bunch of ribs."

"Will my lung and kidney and liver heal? How many ribs did I break?"

He looked thoughtful for a minute. "Bunch of 'em. The organs should heal." He shrugged. "Time will tell."

I was transferred to a room and never saw him again. I urinated blood for several days, and every joint in my body turned black and blue from the internal bleeding, which I later learned was normal.

The question is, in that great moment of trauma, why did my thoughts immediately go to a theology I'd never been taught? There was no debate or fancy Greek words, just death and pending judgment. I never doubted my salvation. I never doubted I'd be seeing Christ in four hours if the doctor was right. But I knew I wouldn't walk into that throne room with my head held high. I wouldn't enter in "confidence," as it says in Hebrews.

Why not? Because I'd lived a polite, American Christian life. There was no passion to rescue the lost from hell; no passion to stand for justice for the oppressed; no passion to serve the needy. I did not pick up my cross daily to serve Christ. Instead I'd done what other people said I should do. I tithed 10 percent out of obligation, did daily devotions, and went to church on Sunday as long as there wasn't something better going on (sometimes the surfing was good). I even attended weekly Bible studies, which was what the really polite American Christians did in the world of which I was a part.

Christian life had been duty without passion, resisting sin without the hatred of it, performing works without love. I was not overcome with gratitude that Jesus was crucified because of my sin; therefore I didn't cry out daily, "Father, let Your will be done on earth as it is in heaven." I was a nice Christian, and nice Christians don't get rewards in heaven because they don't win battles. They don't win battles because they aren't even fighting.

But I didn't answer my own question. Why did my thoughts go to a theology I'd never been taught? Because I had been taught it, but not by a person. The Holy Spirit had been teaching it to me since I dedicated myself to reading Scripture. He is the great teacher—no one else. When facing death, I wasn't thinking of the teaching of Dr. So-and-So, or Pastor What's-His-Name. God's Spirit was making it clear: *You're going to get another chance. Don't miss it. I don't care what Dr. So-and-So says—I care what I say. I told you everything I wanted you to know in My Word, and it clearly says that you will be judged for what you did with the gift of life and salvation I gave you.*

Ephesians 2:8–9 says, "For you are saved by grace through faith, and this is not from yourselves; it is God's gift—not from works, so that no one can boast." That couldn't be simpler or clearer. Even our faith isn't from us. God had to give us the ability to believe in Him. There is nothing about our salvation in which we can take even the least bit of pride. Until that day in the hospital, though, my theology had stopped there, as it does for many people. But while lying on that gurney, the reality of the next verse came crashing through and I was never the same.

Ephesians 2:10 says, "For we are His creation, created in Christ Jesus for good works, which God prepared ahead of time so that we should walk in them." Why were we created? For good works. Not good works that lead to our salvation, but good works *after* our salvation. Before our salvation we were dead. Dead people don't do good works. But when God gave us the gift of faith, allowing us to become alive in Him through His grace, it enabled us to start the reason for our very creation—good works.

But notice the next part of the verse. We were created for good works that were "prepared ahead of time so that we should walk in them." If you are saved, Father has prepared a plan of good works that you are to accomplish. What is the purpose of your life? To accomplish the good works God prepared for you to do long before you drew breath.

How do we know what those are? Understanding and carrying out our reason for living is what most of Christ's teachings are about. Most people will never discover God's plan for themselves because they will not take the narrow road of hard work and suffering, which are the requirements of doing so. They won't risk the criticism of their family and friends. They won't deny themselves the pleasures of this world that get in the way of a relentless pursuit of God's will. They won't live in the delicious uncertainty of daily seeking God's will. They'll instead run after security, pleasure, and comfort.

Some people will pursue God's plan to different extents. And those people will be rewarded to different extents—to the extent of their dedication to His will. This brings us to the judgment seat of Christ. If our sins are forgiven, for what will we be judged?

Jesus says there are the least in His kingdom and those who are great (Matthew 5:19). He says that a cup of cold water given in His name will not be forgotten (Matthew 10:42). Not forgotten to what end? It will not be forgotten when the time for judgment and rewards has come.

He speaks of our being rewarded in a number of ways for what we've done with our lives: we may receive crowns (James 1:12; 1 Corinthians 9:25), become coheirs with Christ (Romans 8:17; Galatians 3:29), co-reign with Him (Matthew 25:21, 2 Timothy 2:11–12), get invited to the wedding feast in heaven (Revelation 19:7–9), get personally congratulated by Him (Matthew 25:21), or even receive a nickname from Him that only we and He will know—a special intimacy between us (Revelation 2:17). These rewards are not guaranteed to all. Some will get them, and some won't. Those who receive them will receive at differing levels according to their walk with Him on earth.

Common themes of those who will be rewarded are obedience, perseverance, suffering, humility or lack of pride, overcoming, faithfulness, and love. Love ties all of them together and is required for the others to have value. God will judge the motivations with which we served Him and others, always looking for love of Him and His people as the foundation. We'll spend some time looking at the rewards later on, what we can win and what it all means, but mostly we'll spend time on what we need to do to win them, just as Jesus did.

I said in the preface that this is supposed to be an encouraging book. But after reading my questioning of modern-day Christianity's standards, you might not be feeling encouraged. It might help to give a brief analogy. Imagine if someone said to you that they'd give you a great reward if you spent an obsessive amount of time with another person of their choosing for two years. You'd need to call them multiple times a day, spend hours on the phone talking about menial things, go out to dinner with them as often as you could afford, attend every event they wanted, and watch the movies or sports teams they chose even though you don't like them. Essentially, you'd need to sacrifice most of what you like to do in order to be with them.

That would be a nightmare. You might do all those things for the allotted time, but it would be a major chore. Yet all those things are exactly what you would do willingly if you were in love with that person. If you're in love, doing those things isn't an obligation; it's a joy. The only difference between the first person and the second is love with passion. Jesus says that the entire law hangs on only two commands—love God with all your heart, and love other people (Matthew 22:36–40).

This book is about having daring faith, and in doing so, you'll receive great rewards. But the message isn't for you to do more—it's for you to fall in love with Jesus. Then the things that now seem like impossible chores will become things of great delight. We will get into detail on the what, the how, and the why as we go through this book. The difficulty or delight of living the life God called us to is in direct proportion to how much we love Him.

THE REST OF THE STORY

You'd think that after the jet ski accident I'd have been more ambitious about serving the Lord, but during the next fourteen years I was lured further into an Americanized way of perceiving a walk with Christ. The message of that day on the gurney never faded, but I got lost in how to do it. I tried a lot harder.

I retired from business at the old age of forty-five in 2012. The business had been massively successful, but success and the financial meltdown brought enemies, lawsuits, and conflict at every turn as ruthless people looked anywhere they could for money and self-promotion. We were one of very few companies that was growing and turning good profits in 2010 and 2011. Running the company seemed more like a daily battle than business. I hated it.

The retirement plan was clear: finish raising our three kids and be in the mountains skiing, hiking, and rafting as much as possible. Over those years, my wife and I gave generously to the church and to the poor. We went on many dangerous mission trips. I preached in third-world countries and saw hundreds receive Christ. I upped my game but didn't change my game. I was trying harder to earn God's approval rather than simply loving Him more, which would translate into passionate obedience to His Word and love for His people.

I had a pretty high opinion of myself as a Christian, and when comparing myself with other comfortable Christians, it was easy to have that opinion. But Christ doesn't tell us to compare ourselves with other people; He tells us to be like Him. He doesn't tell us to give generously; He tells us to give all. Patting ourselves on the back as we compare ourselves to others simply makes us judgmental and insecure. It's just one pig in the slop congratulating itself on being cleaner than the other pigs.

Of course, I planned to volunteer at our church and teach a few classes. I read a lot of great Christian books. It was just what Satan says a good Christian should do. Settle down and make Christianity a hobby.

And then God met me, and it wasn't pleasant. I was praying in a dark closet when Father spoke to me in a more vivid way than ever. You know those mountaintop moments when you are immersed in prayer and He feels so close? This was one of those, but then He got closer than was comfortable.

"Ken, I did not teach you all I did and put you through all I did so you could ski and hike for the rest of your life," He said.

God had never talked to me like this before and He'd never used my name before. I was stunned. "What do You want me to do, Lord?" I asked.

"Are you willing to be as ambitious for My kingdom as you were for your kingdom?" He asked. The question came with a vivid warning. It wasn't spoken; it was simply put in my heart with great force. *Be careful of your answer*, was the warning—*it will cost you your life.*

I didn't want to lose my life. In one of my lesser moments, I answered, "I don't know." Then I started to whine at God. "I'm tired. I'm tired of people, tired of conflict, tired of firing people,

14

tired of being sued. I know the success I've had is all from You: the skills, the situations, the blessings. But haven't I earned the right to take it easy for a while?"

"If you answer no, I'll still bless you," He said, "but you'll miss my full blessing." I had a vision of standing before the judgment seat of Christ. Jesus reviewed my life and showed me what could've been accomplished had I fully died to self. I wept bitterly at the waste of the gifts He'd given.

You'd think that would've been enough, but it still took a long while of wrestling with God before I said, "You know my heart. You know the answer is yes. I'll do whatever You need me to do. If it means losing everything, so be it."

"I'll tell you what I have for you when you're ready." That was all He said. After two hours of wrestling with Him, His final pronouncement was that I wasn't even ready to serve Him yet.

A couple of years went by. I skied and hiked. I read all the books that are too long and complicated to read while one is working: *On the Bondage of the Will* by Luther, *Institutes of the Christian Religion* by Calvin, *City of God* by Augustine, and secular books like *Atlas Shrugged* by Ayn Rand. But now I was impatient. What was God's calling? What was His plan? We'd had this painful moment in which He'd demanded everything, and then He just left me there. Now that I was doing exactly what I used to think happiness was, I was impatient. *If I am going to lay down my life, let's get on with it already.*

My wife, Elliette, is a woman of deep prayer, and she was seeking Father about it. "Ken," she said, "God is speaking to me clearly, and it's just one word—*wait.*"

I didn't like that word. I wanted a different word. Now that the decision had been made, I wanted to get going. Of course, one of the lessons He was teaching was patience. I climbed high into the mountains with a sandwich and thermos of coffee and watched the sun rise and waited to have another conversation with Father. "Lord," I said, "I don't know why You're being so silent after demanding so much, but I'm not leaving this mountain until You tell me what You want. I don't know what I'm going to do if it starts to get dark, but I'm going to read this little Bible I brought up here until You talk to me."

I settled in for a very long day and opened the Bible randomly and started to read. The first verse my eyes went to was Psalm 27:14: "Wait for the LORD; be strong and take heart and wait for the LORD" (NIV).

I just sat there and laughed. God has a sense of humor, and He knew I'd get the joke. He was saying, "Let's not do this all day. I'll just give you the answer now and then you and I can hang out on this mountain." I had the thought of Him saying, "When I said to come to me like a child, I didn't mean like that."

So we hung out. We'd established that He was my Father but also the King, and He'd do what He wanted through me when He wanted. It was a beautiful time on the mountain that day. But little did I know that His will was about to grab my life, and when it did, I'd have no idea it was happening—but that's a story for a different book.

2

CALLED TO MORE THAN SALVATION

For you are saved by grace through faith, and this is not from yourselves; it is God's gift—not from works, so that no one can boast. For we are His creation, created in Christ Jesus for good works, which God prepared ahead of time so that we should walk in them.

EPHESIANS 2:8-10

There are people I'll go to dinner with and people I'll fight shoulder to shoulder with. There are plenty of the first and very few of the second.

CHAD HENNINGS[1]

A MUSLIM EMPLOYEE I WAS WITNESSING TO ONE DAY TOLD me that he could never believe in Christianity because it was so unfair. A Christian had told him once that if someone "accepted Jesus in their heart," it didn't matter if they were a serial killer for the rest of their life—they'd go to heaven and be in paradise forever.

Many people in churches today would agree with this, though they'd feel like something is inherently wrong with the idea. To take it a step further, that serial killer would be in the same heaven as the saints who were burned at the stake for their faith. They'd have the same status as the apostle Paul, who lived a life of suffering to bring the good news of Christ to the world.

That's wrong. The missing piece is that God has shown incredible mercy by doing everything to provide our salvation and forgiveness of sins, but He also will judge us for what we did with that salvation. As you read the following story, you'll feel several emotions. Ask yourself where they're coming from and how they apply to our salvation.

Jake Gordon was a young sergeant in the Los Angeles Police Department in 1968. He was serving in the Internal Affairs Division, which is the team that investigates police officers who have had serious accusations leveled against them.

He and his partner were given a strange case one morning by their lieutenant. It was an accusation against an experienced officer for exposing himself and committing a lewd act outside of a bar in Santa Monica around midnight. The odd part was that the officer had five kids and a happy marriage and had never been in trouble. He was only six months away from his pension—why would he do something so perverse and senseless?

It had to be a false accusation, they'd figured. They went straight to the accused officer. This must be a made-up story—it was the late '60s, after all, and it felt like everyone hated cops. But the officer couldn't help them. He'd gotten blackout drunk and had no recollection of the evening.

"I can't imagine that I'd ever do something like that, fellas," he said, "but I can't remember anything after walking into that bar."

Had he been in a horrible fight with his wife? Did something happen to one of his kids? Did he have a drinking problem? No. A respected policeman with a happy family life had gone down to the beach by himself and sat for several hours, then found himself walking into that bar—and getting completely hammered.

They pressed him. A man doesn't just walk into a bar alone and get blackout drunk. No, he doesn't, the officer agreed. Not unless he'd just been told he had terminal leukemia. Not unless he'd just sat on the beach wondering how he'd tell his wife that their plans of him retiring in six months to raise the kids with her were over. Not unless their dreams of buying a little trailer to camp in the San Gabriel Mountains or up at Big Bear wouldn't happen. Not unless, as he watched the waves roll in, he wondered whether one of his sons might be drafted to fight in Vietnam, and he wouldn't be there to welcome him home afterward.

After all those thoughts hit him in one moment, he ended up passed out near a beach bar. And when he was accused of a lewd act, he had no defense, just shock that anyone would think he could do such a thing.

The complaint had come from two people: a waitress at the bar and her boyfriend, who was waiting outside to pick her up from work. In their story, the boyfriend said he saw the officer walk outside and expose himself, and then his girlfriend walked outside and saw the officer as well. Strangely there were no other witnesses, even though the bar was crowded.

Sergeant Gordon wrote his report, pointing out the inconsistencies with the officer's character and lack of corroborating witnesses. Nevertheless, the officer was fired. Now added to his misery, he'd lost his medical coverage and the pension his wife would need to raise their kids when he was gone. Ironically, due to the lack of supporting witnesses, if he'd simply lied and said it hadn't happened, he would have kept his job. Because of his commitment to truth, he was fired and labeled a pervert.

The young sergeant was unsettled. Something wasn't right, and he asked his lieutenant for permission to continue investigating the case. He received a firm answer—*no*. It was difficult to fire an officer of the LAPD, and having done so was a feather in the lieutenant's cap. It was his ticket to being promoted to captain.

Gordon was convinced that an innocent man and his family were suffering, but he had no proof. No proof until a few months later when he bought a cup of coffee and a bagel in the cafeteria at Parker Center—police headquarters—and opened up the *LA Times*. There was a picture of a young man recently arrested in a grisly triple homicide in Santa Ana. Gordon stared at the photo for a few moments as he processed what he was seeing. It was the young man who had accused the officer.

That night the two Internal Affairs officers drove to the bar in Santa Monica to interview the waitress again. She hesitated at first and then admitted she'd lied—she never saw the officer exposing himself or committing a lewd act. He was just standing outside the bar looking thoroughly drunk. Her boyfriend told her what he'd seen and insisted she back him up—if she didn't, he said he'd kill her. So a terminally ill man sat at home unable to pay for cancer treatments or support his family because he'd been fired—based solely on the word of a man who sat in jail for murder.

Jake Gordon prepared a report that night and excitedly gave it to his lieutenant the next morning, requesting permission to open up the case again. The answer he got sickened him. Not only was he denied, but his commanding officer yelled at him, "Never, in the long and proud history of the LAPD, has a fired officer ever been hired back, and I'm not about to let that happen on my watch!" How could any man let the possibility of a promotion sway him to watch a man's legacy be torn apart and his family destroyed?

The next day the two Internal Affairs officers brought a

department psychologist to the jail to interview the accused murderer. The man was still insistent that he'd seen the officer exposing himself outside the bar that night. The psychologist was able to uncover some serious mental-health issues in the man, mostly stemming from abuse he'd suffered at the hands of his father. And then they got what they needed: the man described his abusive father exposing himself exactly as he'd described the officer doing. When they tracked down a photograph of the father, he looked exactly like the officer.

Case closed. With proof of the officer's innocence, the matter was elevated to Chief Davis, far above Internal Affairs and the lieutenant who ran it. The officer was reinstated and given back pay. To make a happy ending even happier, he beat cancer, and he and his wife enjoyed a long retirement together.

It was a happy ending for everyone—except Gordon. His lieutenant was incensed and promised revenge. Only a month later, the young sergeant found himself transferred from his prestigious position at Internal Affairs to walking a foot beat in downtown Los Angeles, rousting heroin addicts and chasing down car burglars. His diligence to truth and justice had seriously cost him. While he got stuck at sergeant, he watched an evil man get promoted to captain—and then commander.

JUSTICE

How does that story strike you? Jake Gordon was a well-known Christian on the LAPD, who had made quite a mark on the department when it came to racial equality. He told me that story in 1989 when I was a young officer on the LAPD. By then he had made it all the way up to captain, but it had taken him longer than it should have, which kept him from getting to commander. He was probably the most respected captain on the department. To make matters worse, they made an episode of *Police Story*, a '70s TV show on NBC, about the incident. Jake's partner had sold the story and pocketed a check, and young Sergeant Gordon never saw a dime.

My reaction to the story was righteous anger. Where was the justice? Where was fairness? We have built into us a natural sense of right and wrong. There is a way things are supposed to go, and when someone violates that, harming others for their own gain, we demand that something be done about it. Sergeant Gordon had risked all to stand up for the fired officer, but would it be made right?

We've been taught an almost communistic foundation to the gospel: If you say a prayer, you're in the "club"—the salvation club—and you can never be thrown out of it. When you die, you'll go to heaven. Jesus will meet you with a big smile and give you a tour and introduce you to Peter and the boys, the apostle Paul, Moses, Abraham, and beautiful Esther. We'll all hang out at a wedding feast and watch the fight on earth while Jesus finally throws the devil into the lake of fire.

Maybe it wasn't said so cynically, but that is the gist of what is understood by too many Christians today. We are told that Jesus did it all on the cross, and our salvation is in no way dependent on works; therefore, we should try to be good people because that makes Jesus happy, but it really doesn't matter. If you do wicked things, stop feeling bad. The only real sin left anymore is feeling bad about your sin.

People are checking out of the church in droves. They're checking out of the evangelical churches, the Catholic churches, the charismatic churches, and, most of all, the liberal Protestant churches. If life is pointless once a person has prayed the magic prayer, why wouldn't they? If the only reason to go to church, help the poor, give generously, sacrifice our rights for others, and seek holiness is because Jesus would really like us to, then we'll get what has been growing within the church for decades now—people trying to do nice things in their own power without complete surrender to God's Spirit. There is little death to self, perseverance, or true generosity because there are no real consequences; it's simply us doing a favor for the Creator of the universe. Aren't we nice?

We've taught a weak and feckless Jesus who runs a weak and feckless religion. But we've been lied to. Jesus came to earth as the Lamb to be slaughtered for our sins, but He is now a victorious King. He will hand out judgment to the unbelievers and to the believers. The unbelievers will face judgment at the great white throne and will face eternal separation from God (Revelation 20:11–15). Believers will face judgment at a different throne—the judgment seat of Christ, called the bema seat (2 Corinthians 5:10; 1 Corinthians 3:11–15), where they will be rewarded for their works, receive crowns, or in some cases face consequences for wasted lives.

As we run through the emotions of Gordon's story, we see

that he will receive justice for what he did by our Father in good time. Though he suffered in this life, he will receive great reward for standing firm for what is right. God is a God of both justice and mercy. His mercy was limitless in the forgiveness of our sins. His justice will be rendered for those whose sins are forgiven by rewarding those who stood firm, despite the temporal cost.

THE LIAR

We must always remember that the enemy of our souls, Satan, prowls around like a roaring lion seeking someone to devour (1 Peter 5:8). His best tool is that he is the master liar, as he is the Father of Lies (John 8:44). The best lie is the one closest to the truth. Actually, even better is the truth itself given in a way that leads a person to the wrong conclusion. If you have given your life to Christ, you are lost to Satan. The best he can do now is to convince you not to be effective in building God's kingdom.

Jesus did it all on the cross with His death and resurrection. But what do we mean by *all*? He provided the path for the forgiveness of our sins. As we see in the verse that starts this chapter, we had nothing to do with our salvation from sins, so we can boast in nothing. As the Reformers who gave their lives to change the corrupt church claimed, *"sola fide"*—faith alone is what saves us; works have nothing to do with it.

But in the lie—the true statement that leads to the wrong

conclusion—that He did it all, we forget the rest of the phrase above. All of our salvation was accomplished by Christ, but we were saved for a reason. We were saved for good works. Not just any good works—works specifically prepared for each of us to accomplish at the beginning of time. God had you in mind when He laid the foundations of the world. He knew your every sin—every jealous, bitter, murderous, envious, lustful thought—and He forgave them all. He did it because, despite the sinful nature in you, He would seal you as His child when you believed, by putting a part of Himself in you—His Holy Spirit.

Jesus did it all, not to get you to the end, but to get you to the beginning. You were dead; now, if you've put your faith in Christ, you are alive. You are born again. You are a baby who must now grow into an adult. And as you become an adult, He has work for you to do.

Either that Spirit will grow in you as you turn from sin and grow in Him, enabling you to accomplish the works He planned for you to do, or that Spirit will not grow because you choose selfishness, pride, and sin, and you won't accomplish the tasks He predestined for you. Make no mistake about it, we will be rewarded for completing the tasks God gave us at the beginning of creation, and we will suffer loss for those we didn't.

Unless we as members of the body of Christ are studying His Word and then coming together to worship and be taught by a pastor who we insist is qualified and uncompromising in his teaching, we are open to the lies of the devil—many are so tiny we don't even notice them—each designed to pull us off the narrow path. Just a little, just enough to begin concluding the wrong things.

One of the astronauts from the '60s told me once that his spacecraft was off course 99 percent of the time on its way to orbit the moon. It was the tiny and constant corrections all along the way that got it to where it needed to be. So it is with us, except for one major difference—his spacecraft didn't have a devil trying desperately to hinder and keep it off track. Therefore, we must be diligent every moment of every day to guard our souls and to gather regularly with godly brothers and sisters who will sharpen us and hold us accountable.

THE REST OF THE STORY

John, a young firefighter in Southern California, was called to a prestigious community to help an unresponsive eighty-seven-year-old man. On the ride to the hospital, the old man became semiconscious and began mumbling. His eyes were panicked and filled with fear.

The young firefighter leaned down to comfort the man and was surprised at the haunting things coming from his mouth. The man was going through nightmares. Worse than nightmares—because these were true. The old man recounted a life of cowardice. He moaned on in regret over detailed acts of cowardice and betrayal. His life was one of arrogance and misery.

As the man recounted his life in stories, John realized that the man had been a commander in the LAPD, a very powerful position. How, John wondered, could such a disgraceful man have been promoted so high? Strangely, one of the stories sounded vaguely familiar. He couldn't place it, but it struck him like a long-lost memory.

When work ended, John decided to call his father, retired captain Jake Gordon, to ask him about the man. "It was weird, Dad," he said. "This guy's own stories showed him to be one of the most despicable cowards I'd ever seen. I couldn't believe he was an LAPD cop."

Captain Gordon, ever slow to say anything critical about anyone else, finally told John who that commander was. "Remember, son, the story about the officer with leukemia I fought to get rehired? Remember the lieutenant who stabbed me in the back? John, that old man was the lieutenant."

Two days later, John transported someone to the same hospital and checked the log to see if the old commander was still admitted. He was. The young firefighter walked into the room and looked him over. The man's wife and son sat in the corner. "He had coward's eyes, Ken," he said as he told me the story. "You know those eyes that are soft and fearful but also full of rage? Kind of like they're trying to decide whether to run or shoot you in the back?" I nodded; I knew that look all too well.

John told the old man that he'd come to check on him. As they talked, it was clear that the man didn't recall what he'd said on the trip to the hospital. As John got ready to leave, he looked down at the miserable old coward. "My dad was an

LAPD cop—same time as you. You must have known him. His name was Jake Gordon."

The man looked like he'd been slapped, then paused, looking back in fear. He furrowed his brow. "Nope, doesn't ring a bell."

John looked down on him with sadness. "Well, he said he'll never forget you." The old man died a few days later, his last chance at redemption drowned by his pride.

CALLED TO BE COURAGEOUS

Be alert, stand firm in the faith, act like a man, be strong.

1 CORINTHIANS 16:13

The core virtue of a coward is niceness.
You must lick the boot that kicks you.

TIM DUNN[1]

THOMAS CRANMER WAS A COWARD AND A TRAITOR TO Jesus Christ, but I wonder if I'm anywhere near the man that he was.

My daughter, Ashton, and I stood in Christ Church, a medieval cathedral in Oxford, England. I'd taken Ashton to Paris, Copenhagen, and Prague on a business trip because, at twelve, she was already a prolific reader and budding intellectual. I'd read her The Chronicles of Narnia and *The Hobbit* when she was little, so she'd convinced me to add London and Oxford to the trip so she could walk in the footsteps of G. K. Chesterton, C. S. Lewis, and J. R. R. Tolkien.

In the cathedral was a notch in a stone pillar. Above the notch was a sign that this was where they had built the altar where Cranmer was to kneel, recanting his teaching about the grace of Jesus. I knew the story. It was a foregone conclusion— Cranmer, the coward who watched his two friends burned at the stake, had never missed an opportunity to be weak. But Cranmer wasn't going to be weak this time; he wouldn't need the altar. Instead he was going to shock the world.

Thomas Cranmer had made several bold reforms under King Edward. He was a stalwart for the reformation of the church and wrote many bold policies against the established Catholic Church while serving as the archbishop of Canterbury. His boldness had come while there was a monarch on the throne who agreed with him. Then an inconvenient thing happened: Edward died, and Bloody Mary came to the throne.

Mary got her name because of the slaughter she instigated against those who were perceived as enemies of the Catholic Church, and Cranmer was at the top of her list. Cranmer was put on trial with two other Reformers, Hugh Latimer and Nicholas Ridley. Following the trial, Latimer and Ridley were immediately burned alive while Cranmer was forced to watch. Latimer died almost immediately from the smoke.

Ridley died slowly. The wood around him wouldn't ignite well and he burned for a long time before dying. He cried out for someone to put more wood under him to hasten his death. Cranmer, horrified by watching their murders, couldn't seem to write enough letters recanting everything he'd stood for to avoid the same fate. Cranmer was given the opportunity to publicly refute everything he had preached about the grace of Christ, and he took it.

As Cranmer entered the cathedral that Ashton and I stood in 450 years later, he began to preach the sermon everyone expected. But when he was supposed to recant his teachings, he instead affirmed them, denying everything he'd written in trying to save himself and condemning the hand that had written such things.

Cranmer was ripped from the pulpit and rushed past the altar where he was to kneel as a coward and out to where his friends were murdered six months earlier. As the flames raged, Cranmer placed his right hand into them so that the instrument he'd used to deny the truth of Christ would burn first.

What gives a man such boldness? How does a person move from a history of opportunism and cowardice to such immense bravery? It's appropriate for us to ask ourselves whether we could bear up under such circumstances as Cranmer, Latimer, and Ridley. Would we stand strong? As the flames raged, would we climb onto the stake and be burned to avoid compromising the truth of Christ?

Revelation 21:8 gives us a list of those whose "share will be in the lake that burns with fire and sulfur." Revelation 20 has already assured us that only those whose names are not written in the Book of Life will be condemned to the lake of fire, so the list in 21:8 is a warning to all who have lived a life typified by certain actions that testify they aren't truly believers. There is an entire chapter devoted to this near the end of this book, but it's helpful to discuss a brief part of it here.

Here is the list of actions. I've blanked one out; let's see if you can guess what it is. "But the _____, unbelievers, vile, murderers, sexually immoral, sorcerers, idolaters, and all liars—their share will be in the lake that burns with fire." Since salvation is a gift based on God's grace and comes to us only through belief and through no merit of our own, the list above is clearly stating that anyone whose life is typified by such actions doesn't truly believe in Jesus.

So what is the one action I blanked out? Is it being a thief? A greedy person? An addict? No, none of those. The person who starts the list of those who the Bible says will go to the lake of fire for eternity, who are not saved, is the coward.

Cowards? Really? When was the last time you heard a

sermon on not being a coward? Yet the Bible lists it as one of the eight sins for which, if you are typified by them, you are guaranteed to be condemned. It isn't just on the list; it starts the list.

Notice that everything on the list, except for cowardice, is a definable thing. Lying is telling something that is not the truth. A murderer takes another's life without justification. But what defines cowardice? Cowardice is disobeying God's commands because of fear. For instance, if a person refuses to stand up against abortion because they're worried about losing their job or being unpopular—that's cowardice. It doesn't necessarily make one a coward if it doesn't typify one's life, but if fear for one's reputation keeps them from standing up for helpless babies in the womb, that person might want to take a serious assessment of their life and wonder if they're a coward.

I remember committing a cowardly act while preaching to a large crowd in Asia many years ago. It was in a poor, high-crime area, and several thousand people came to hear the message on salvation. We had a great altar call, and many people came forward to publicly place their faith in Christ. As I was down in the crowd praying for people, an older woman came hobbling toward me, supported by a teenage girl. "Preacher," the girl said, "my grandma is crippled, and she wants you to ask God to heal her."

I wasn't "that kind" of preacher. I had no idea what to do. The old woman, who clearly didn't speak English, just stood there, smiling hopefully. The young girl politely stood several yards away while I got on my knees to pray.

My heart went out to the woman and her granddaughter who'd come to hear the gospel, but I was really at a loss of what to do. "Lord," I prayed, "You and I both know I don't have any idea what to do right now. But if You don't heal this lady, You and I are really going to look stupid. Would You heal her despite my inadequacy? Don't withhold a miracle from her because of my unworthiness." (That's exactly what I prayed.)

The woman got healed. She leaped away from me and started screaming and praising God. She started bouncing and dancing, far more than anyone her age should have been able to. It attracted a crowd—and I got away from there. I hopped onstage and walked into the back where no one else could ask for a miracle.

I ran away and hid. Even though the Lord had shown He would do something amazing despite my inadequacy, my faith failed. Days later, I realized that He may have been ready to pour out His Spirit in an unbelievable way. We may have seen miracles beyond imagination—I'll never know, because I walked away. I kept thinking of that hopeful look on her face and was relieved that she hadn't been disappointed, but I was unwilling to risk it again. My faith was too little and pride too much, such that I didn't realize the obvious, which was that someone's healing was completely up to Him. All He was asking was that I obey and act as His vessel—and I walked away.

It was an act of cowardice, and many people may have been robbed of a blessing because of me. Am I a coward? No. But I definitely needed to repent of cowardice and pray for those who may have lost out on a blessing because of my inaction.

Courage is the opposite of cowardice and similarly vague. Courage is obeying God's commands despite fear. Courage is valuing obedience to God's Word more than whatever the consequences from the world might be. In fact, the more fear one has, yet obeys anyway, the more courage one displays.

When I was serving on the Los Angeles Police Department, I noticed that character separated the good police officers from the bad ones. But it was courage that separated the good officers from the great ones. We had a saying on the LAPD about cowardly officers: they were first in line to eat and last in line to die.

The most repeated command in the Bible is to not fear. It's a command, not a suggestion. But can we actually control whether we are fearful? Yes. God doesn't command something that is impossible to obey. Controlling fear comes through exercising courage. The more one obeys God's Word, despite fear, the less control fear has. Soon a mature believer finds that the things that once seemed intimidating are now invigorating. It can be scary to share the good news of Jesus to a stranger, but after one does it several times, fear turns to excitement. Sharing your faith turns from a chore to a delight.

Have you noticed that there are people who seem terrified all the time? They obsess over every news story, every sickness, every possible risk. Have you also noticed that there are those rare people who never seem to be afraid of anything? There are things that lead to a life filled with fear and there are things that lead to a life of fearlessness. I've noticed another thing—fear and misery go together, and so do fearlessness and joy.

The COVID-19 scare revealed a lot about humanity. We watched as many churches closed their doors and refused to open. Even while bars, strip clubs, and casinos opened so that people could feed their addictions, churches stayed closed. When I filmed a call to pastors to open their church doors to meet the needs of the hungry, the suicidal, and the dying, I received a torrent of responses from Christians with lectures on how reckless that was, and the video was banned from social media. This, while restaurants were open and nearly all the churches were closed. Some churches did stay open during that time, and those pastors are to be respected.

Was Covid something to be concerned about? Of course. Some of my close friends came very near death. People who I knew died. Gene Getz, a dear friend and member of the Promise Keepers pastors board, was in the hospital for eight months with Covid and had to learn to walk again when he got out. But during that time, I also knew people who died of cancer, car accidents—one was stabbed to death. Yet I was never lectured by Christians about closing churches due to the possibility that someone might die on their drive to church or meet a knife-wielding maniac while walking into the service. You might think that's a silly comparison . . . what are the odds of being murdered in America or dying in a car accident? Depending on which data one uses—about the same as dying from Covid.

So what leads to fearlessness? Faith. It's faith in the fact that our heavenly Father's will is perfect, and we strive to be part of it—even if it costs us.

That's why fearlessness and joy go together. Because the soul that has placed utter and complete faith in Jesus Christ is the soul that obeys Him despite risk. It begins by believing in Jesus and the free gift of His salvation and forgiveness of sins, which leads to repentance and a changing of our ways. It is completed as we grow in Him and learn to die to ourselves and the mistaken belief that we have a right to our life. We have no right to our own life; we gave that up when we placed our faith in Jesus.

As we were relaunching Promise Keepers, I had many calls from leaders all over the world. Most were great, a few were discouraging. One man, the CEO of a major ministry, asked me to lunch. As we talked about the vision of the new Promise Keepers, he said, "Man, where did you get so much courage?"

I thought about that for a minute. "Why do you say I have courage?" I asked.

"I could never do what you're doing. The task you've taken on is enormous! Don't you see how bold that is?"

His statement made me sad. He meant it as a compliment, of course, but the larger implication was disturbing. Thinking of that notch in the pillar in Oxford, I said, "If I failed at bringing back Promise Keepers, what would happen to me?"

He thought about that as I continued. "All that would happen is that I'd look really stupid. Some people I don't know would say, 'Wow, that Ken Harrison guy failed. What a loser!' Is this our idea of boldness in the church today? Our forefathers were burned, skinned alive, and sawn in two, but our modern-day American view of boldness is that I risk looking bad. Man, I hope we increase our view of boldness."

Will we have what it takes to stand firm in our faith when persecution comes? We in the West (Europe and the United States) have been raised in an environment where society was Christian in its worldview. But throughout the history of the world since Christ, this has been the exception, not the rule. As we see the Western world descend into deep rebellion against Christ and into sexual perversion, which always leads to violence and persecution of the innocent, will we stand strong?

As we give away our life to Him, faith grows, and we realize that whatever happens to us is His will—and we delight in it. We understand that we will all die, whether in a car wreck, or at the hands of a murderer, or from Covid—and it doesn't matter, because it is His will. We begin to understand that salvation is a free gift but it costs us everything. As we grow in this realization and as we grow in trusting the goodness of our Father, we find that fear diminishes and with it comes great freedom and a life of joy.

Thus we see that the opposite of faith is what leads to fear. When we don't fully trust in God, when we hold back parts of our lives, fear takes root. I've often been quoted as saying that humility is the outward expression of a person who is truly in love with Jesus. The negative side of that statement is also true: fear is the sign of someone whose life is not wholly dedicated to Jesus.

There is only one path to joy. There is only one road to being the kind of person who rejoices when their possessions are unjustly taken away or when they're thrown into prison and suffer great loss. That is complete abandonment to Christ.

That is having our eyes fixed on Him and only Him. No one else's opinion matters, only our Father's, who gave His all to redeem us from our sins. With our eyes fixed on Him in faith, we walk that narrow road that leads to eternal life, even if it means pain and death in this life.

Refuse to be held hostage anymore to the fear that robs you from the joy-filled life that Jesus created you for. Evangelist Leonard Ravenhill had this question inscribed on his gravestone: "Are the things you are living for worth Christ dying for?"[2] Fear says no. Faith says absolutely!

THE REST OF THE STORY

As Hugh Latimer and Nicholas Ridley burned at the stake and Thomas Cranmer looked on, Latimer looked over at his friend and said, "Be of good comfort, Master Ridley, and play the man; we shall this day light such a candle by God's grace in England as shall never be put out."[3]

And so they did. The examples of the martyrdom of Latimer, Ridley, and Cranmer would indeed ignite a candle in England. Many giants of the faith came in rapid succession after their deaths, from John Wesley to Charles Spurgeon, from William Wilberforce to Oswald Chambers. Maybe the greatest preacher in history also came out of their example— George Whitefield.

Not all courage is staring down evil or fighting for justice. Sometimes it is faith in the face of suffering. Courage and humility walk together. When a person values others as more important than themselves (Philippians 2:3), it has a remarkable effect on their willingness to sacrifice all out of love for others.

George Whitefield was one of the most famous preachers in the world when he boarded a ship to the American colonies. On the way to America, deadly sickness broke out on the ship. Whitefield spent the journey nursing the sick, and by the time they landed at the colony of Georgia, he was severely ill. Whitefield's ministry was delayed for two weeks while he recovered. Whitefield could easily have justified sequestering himself because he was on a major spiritual mission. He could have left the work to people who were gifted in that area. Instead, considering others as more important than himself, he suffered greatly in order to serve.

The result? Whitefield, along with his friend Jonathan Edwards, fathered the Great Awakening, probably the greatest revival in the history of the world. Whitefield was a man utterly abandoned in his passion to serve Christ. He persevered through terrible sicknesses and trials and exercised patience to the extent that even Benjamin Franklin marveled at his dedication to the faith.

God loves people who completely trust Him, even when they might suffer. The key is learning to live in the moment and wait on God. For us to be courageous to the point of a daring faith, we must first have the certainty that we're in His will. As we'll see in the next chapter, when we have the courage to truly walk with Him, God invites us to be His friends.

4

CALLED TO BE GOD'S FRIEND

And whenever you turn to the right or to the left, your ears will hear this command behind you: "This is the way. Walk in it."

ISAIAH 30:21

We can't explain a movement of the Spirit. The more we try to explain it, the more we miss it.

JAMES ROBISON[1]

ONE OF THE FIRST TIMES I MET WITH JAMES ROBISON WAS in a restaurant near Fort Worth, Texas. We'd met once or twice before. James was a well-known evangelist and TV personality. We had seen God's Spirit in each other and immediately became close friends. As we sat down, a waitress in her midtwenties excitedly handed him an envelope filled with cash. It was her tips from the day before. She was giving to help build a well for the poor in Africa. James clearly ate at this restaurant all the time; it seemed as if the entire staff greeted him warmly.

I talked with the waitress alone for a few minutes. She told me James had led her to Christ, and she'd then led her mother to Christ. "He's led many here to Christ," she said. "Everyone who works here is a Christian now." As I expressed my amazement, she told me he'd led many of their customers to Christ as well. "Sometimes during dinner, Mr. Robison stands and starts preaching. He does an altar call here sometimes!"

"You guys don't stop him?" I asked.

"Oh no," she said. "We owe our lives to James Robison."

I've had the chance to see his passion for the things of God many times. James constantly amazes me with the godly wisdom that he displays. He has a relationship with God that is closer than anyone else's I've known. James seems to hear straight from God. The question is why, and how can we be like that too?

The first sixteen years of James's life were marked by hunger, bouts of homelessness, and suffering. One of the few times James Robison had a conversation with his father was looking down the barrel of his new hunting rifle. Hunger and poverty were closer to James than his father, so his dad sat very carefully in the chair. He knew that James's relationship with his rifle was much stronger than with the man at whom it was pointed.

James's father looked into the boy's eyes and knew he'd be justified if he pulled the trigger. He was a drunk and a rapist. It was that last part that was the reason James existed—actually, it was both. James's mother had been a nurse providing hospice care to a dying man. A poor, scared forty-year-old childless woman raped by the man's drunken son, who left her screaming and battered—and pregnant.

Abortions were hard to come by in 1943 but not impossible, and James's mother was looking for one. James was born because the doctor she found refused to kill him. Destitute and scared, she didn't know what to do, and that's when James's real Father spoke to her. *Do not terminate this baby*, He told her. *The child will bring joy to the world.* When the rapist showed up to victimize the mother once again, he found that the baby had turned into fourteen-year-old James and his hunting rifle.

But only a few years later, James Robison was on his way to becoming one of the greatest evangelists who ever walked the earth. He was filling football stadiums across the United States. He preached with a fiery passion that called hundreds of thousands forward to give their lives to Jesus. It was James who was dispatched by the leaders of the evangelical church to talk Ronald Reagan into running for president in 1979. It was James who everyone pronounced was to be the next Billy Graham, selling out stadiums into his nineties, just like Billy. Everyone, that is, except his real Father.

James had a lesson to learn, and he was not going to rise to his calling until he learned it. Fresh off talking the newly elected President Reagan into running, James called his friend and mentor Billy Graham to give him a lecture. James didn't approve of some of the preachers Billy was associating with. "Do you know any of these people you're criticizing, James?" Billy asked.

James didn't. Billy asked James to spend a weekend with Oral Roberts, a well-known preacher from a different denomination. To James, Oral was one of "those people" who believe "that stuff," nothing that should separate us as brothers and sisters in Christ, but which so often has. The church at the time of James's lecture to Billy was divided into a few main "tribes." Two of the biggest were the fundamentalists and the charismatics. James was a leader of the fundamentalists and Oral of the charismatics.

Since then, the church has divided into so many tribes with finger-pointing, backstabbing, and gossiping in the name of Jesus that our Father surely looks at us in sad disappointment. He told us to be one as Jesus and the Father are one so we could rescue people from the grasp of hell. Instead we divide churches over how to serve communion, the proper way to baptize, or even the color of the carpet. When I was a boy, I remember the two scandals that rocked Tri-City Baptist

Temple. One was whether women should be allowed to wear pants to church (seriously), and the other was that some radicals wanted to bring a piano into the church alongside the organ. Our scandals are different today, but just as sinful, as they keep us from being about our Father's business. The suicidal, the addict, the abused, the confused . . . they don't care whether our theology is perfect; they need to know there is hope for them. They need the Savior.

"Those people" who believe "that stuff" was exactly what James was lecturing Billy about. James did spend that weekend with Oral, and it changed his life. In the early 1980s, Oral Roberts was one of the most famous televangelists in the world. He'd built an empire in Tulsa, Oklahoma. He was idolized by those from his tribe and vilified by those outside.

"I'm so lonely, James," Oral told him. "I'm under so much pressure and judged from all sides. The world on one side, the church on the other side. I have no one I can talk to."

James was touched. Oral was just a man. A very gifted man, but just a man. James became lifelong friends with Oral, and then he began to seek out Christian leaders from the other denominations he'd been taught to avoid. He found godly leaders with different views on some Bible passages who taught and blessed him greatly. It was only a matter of time before his own "side" started questioning him, then criticizing him—just as he'd criticized Billy Graham. What was he doing with "those people"? Had he lost his way?

At the height of James's fame, God called him to stop preaching and start a television show with his wife, Betty. This was odd. He was the most famous preacher in the world besides Billy Graham and still thought to be the next "anointed one." But God's ways are not ours. With his television show, James was able to promote and financially support many of the leaders and leading ministries of today, including Promise Keepers. He has become one of the biggest supporters of clean water initiatives in Africa.

By stepping off the stage, James gave up power and fame. He knew that Billy Graham was aging, and James would be the man filling stadiums worldwide. The new man that presidents would come to for approval from the church. Instead he stepped behind the scenes to become a unifier and promoter of others' ministries.

The boy conceived in rape and raised in squalor with no father in his life had become a great evangelist, only to trade stadiums for restaurant tables. God became James's friend because he walked in obedience. James has three children, eleven grandchildren, and fourteen great-grandchildren. He is the most blessed and content person I've ever known. He has only one burning desire—to build God's kingdom by sharing the gospel and unifying the church.

We hear much in today's culture about the status of one's birth. Some are born with more privilege than others. They get a head start in this world. But when it comes to being called God's friend, one's earthly birth status doesn't matter—only his or her born-again status matters, and in that we all begin life equally. James Robison doesn't wonder what God wants; his Father tells him because they're friends. Jesus says we can be friends with Him. We can know Him so well that He directs our paths without our even being aware because we abide in Him so closely. How do we do that?

SLAVE OR FRIEND

"You are My friends if you do what I command you" (John 15:14 NASB).

Jesus pronounced to His apostles that they were no longer slaves, but His friends. Imagine Messiah, the Creator of all things, telling you that you are His friend. Imagine the apostles, traveling with Him day and night, seeing the dead raised, the diseased healed, the hungry fed from thin air, suddenly told that they are His friends.

Jesus was calling them into a higher level of relationship. The twelve men who had been considered slaves to Him, not knowing what His will was, were now called to higher relationship—to friendship and an inclusion into His will. Jesus would now begin trusting them with details about what was to come and how they fit into His plan (John 15:15).

What had they done to warrant such a vulnerable and loving closeness to God? They had obeyed Him, they had suffered with Him, and they had persevered. Jesus had already watched many of His followers leave Him. So much so that He turned to the Twelve and asked, "You don't want to go away too, do you?" (John 6:67). Peter's answer: "Lord, who will we go to? . . . You are the Holy One of God!" (vv. 68–69).

Jesus' first promise to them after pronouncing them His

friends was that they would be hated. Because He chose them out of the world, the world would hate them. Don't let this slip by casually. The world is full of people who haven't given their lives to Jesus. Whether they are aware of it or not, they are hostile to the things of God because they are still dead in their sins.

For many people, the world is their own wife or husband, their children, their parents, and siblings. So it is with everyone who wishes to be at such a level of closeness with Jesus that He would deem them a friend. He must be first. Before every relationship, before every desire, we must pursue Him relentlessly. If we do, we will find an intimacy with Him we never thought possible.

Look again at the verse that starts this chapter. "And whenever you turn to the right or to the left, your ears will hear this command behind you: 'This is the way. Walk in it'" (Isaiah 30:21). Sometimes it's hard to believe that God would instruct us like that. There are promises in God's Word that we gloss over because they seem impossible. But they are possible to those few who are completely abandoned to knowing Christ, to those willing to lose themselves to do their part to bring His kingdom to the world.

The keys are passion, perseverance, and patience. Passion in loving Him—which means loving what He loves and hating what He hates. What does He love? He loves people. He has special affection for the oppressed and the suffering. He loves justice. He loves humility. He loves holiness. What does He hate? He hates pride (1 Peter 5:5). He hates seeing people used and taken advantage of. He hates a lack of faith (Hebrews 10:38).

PASSION

A good exercise in understanding God's nature is a study of Isaiah. It's amazing how often God declared what He loves and what He hates. Isaiah was the prophet who received the incredible revelation about the coming Messiah. Yet instead of starting with that, God started by declaring what He loves: "Learn to do what is good. Seek justice. Correct the oppressor. Defend the rights of the fatherless. Plead the widow's cause" (1:17).

Notice these are all actions. Learning to do what is good is a lifelong pursuit of seeking Him and studying His Word. The next four are all actions that require faith and courage and will make enemies for us—just as Jesus promised. Seeking justice means putting ourselves in the crosshairs of those who need justice, which are often bullies and violent people. Being a justice seeker can get us fired, kicked out of our social groups, or sued.

Being able to look a hostile person in the eye and speak truth in love is hard. It's much easier to say nothing and pretend we're just "staying out of it." Remaining neutral in the face of injustice and evil is for cowards, not something for the people of God. Someone said to me, regarding an argument between two ministry leaders we knew, "Well, you know, there's always three sides to every argument: one side, the other side, and the truth." I corrected him immediately. Sometimes there are just two sides: the truth and the lie. The coward says there are three sides so he can "stay out of it" and pretend he's keeping the peace. They are the peacekeepers instead of the peacemakers.

Please remember we're talking about correcting the oppressor. Isaiah was not saying that we need to insert ourselves into every argument. He was saying only that we need to insert ourselves when someone is being wronged. We're to correct the oppressor, not the person with a different opinion. Defending widows and orphans (which in the ancient world meant the broader definition of the oppressed) means taking our neighbors and friends to right wrongs.

PERSEVERANCE

All these things risk creating conflict, making enemies, and inviting hatred. This brings us to the second thing required in becoming God's friend: perseverance. Risking these things in the moment is hard. Risking them for a lifetime is impossible without Father holding us up. Sometimes there is a brief victory. We correct the oppressor, and when they repent, we have restored a brother or sister. Sometimes we defend the widow, and we see justice. But most of the time we will not witness justice being served, at least not in the short term.

The fight to end slavery by John Newton and William Wilberforce took decades. The fight for civil rights took a century. The fight to take sexual assaults on women seriously took many years. In every case, it took relentless perseverance through being mocked, jailed, and sued before we saw success. The fight to end abortion has been the same, and many people have suffered in it but have never quit. Many of the great saints who fought for justice never saw victory in their lifetimes. They fought for future generations. Even in failure they never stopped. They persevered.

So many people quit just before victory. Many people can be passionate for a brief time, but they wither in the daily grind of the fight. It takes a special person to stay passionate for a lifetime, especially when all they see in the moment is defeat. They quit a project. They quit the faith. They quit their families. God rewards those who persevere with a crown (James 1:12). Humbly seek the Lord, and if He is in your plans, He will give you success in His time, not yours.

PATIENCE

The King James Version of the Bible typically uses the word *longsuffering* for patience. That's a great word for it. The Holy Spirit's favorite word is *wait*. Wait—you aren't ready to accomplish His purposes. Wait—He's doing many things for many people and your time to act or speak isn't yet. Wait—He's working on the people you are to minister to, and their hearts aren't prepared. In my own story of climbing a mountain and insisting God reveal His will, I wanted Him to work in my time. What I was to learn was that He was waiting for me to mature. He knew that as I relaunched Promise Keepers, I would be attacked in the media and by other Christians and have death threats made against me to try to silence the message He'd given. I was in no way ready for that on the mountain that day.

I still needed to learn many things, not the least of which was to wait on Him.

How much damage well-meaning Christians have done because they rushed ahead of God! Art Remington, Promise Keepers's pastor for twenty-five years, has a saying: "Make sure you never see your shadow [from running ahead of God's glory]." Moses had a great call on His life but grew tired of waiting on God and caused great destruction in his life. So each of us has a great call, which can only glorify Father and be completely effective in His time. Our pride and the voice of the devil are in a hurry. God is never in a hurry.

We see, then, that becoming God's friend is the opposite of cultural Christianity. It is not attending church once a week (though that is part of it), sitting passively in a seat, and being a nice person the rest of the week. Instead it is action. (Seek justice. Correct the oppressor.) It is exhortation. It is relentless work to be used by Father to bring as much of His kingdom on earth as we are able. It is always keeping Ephesians 2:10 at the forefront of our minds—that we were created for good works, which were prepared beforehand.

THE REST OF THE STORY

Years ago I was sitting on a Southwest Airlines flight when a very elderly man sat next to me. I didn't yet know James Robison and was only beginning to hear God's voice. It was the beginning of learning to become His friend and hear His will clearly. As usual on flights, I just wanted to put my headphones on, read, and listen to music. Instead I felt that gentle nudging from the Lord to witness to the man. It was a fascinating conversation as he told me about his life as an astronaut. He and I became friends.

A few months later I flew across the country to really witness to him, and we spent five hours together at an oceanfront restaurant talking about Christ and the cosmos. At one point, while explaining why having spacecraft take off from Florida is more difficult than from Russia, he wrote out a long mathematical formula and said impatiently, "See? It's obvious."

I looked at rows of math and chuckled. "My degree is in English literature," I said. "I can quote you Shakespeare, but I can't read that." I still have that paper and warm memories of him. He told amazing stories of the beginning of the space program, of the race with Russia to space, and hair-raising stories of the possibilities of being stuck in space. But after five hours of very pleasant conversation, in which he agreed with the truth of just about everything I said, he was nowhere close to receiving Christ.

It was confusing. I was armed with all the scientific facts, and he delighted in talking about them. He talked about how all he saw in space was black everywhere, and then there was this little blue ball with light shining on it, and he knew there must be something special about that blue ball. We discussed God, creation, depravity, and grace, and he nodded along, agreeing with it all. Asked whether he'd like to go a little further and receive Christ, he politely declined.

Afterward I drove to the beach and asked God why. Why would he agree with the facts but reject the truth? *Because he doesn't think he needs a Savior*, I heard the Lord say. My heart broke for him. He'd been at the top. Everyone who knew him respected him. But his pride was so great that he could agree the masses needed a Savior while he did not.

James Robison, almost aborted, raised in squalor with a rapist for a father, became God's friend. He became a man blessed greatly because he was abandoned to all that God had. When James stands before Jesus at the end of his days, he will be greeted by hundreds of thousands of friends, because of James's obedience. The man born with nothing was declared a friend of God and will receive all the joy on earth and crowns in heaven that come with it.

And the greatly respected astronaut, whom the world lauded, who had accomplished so much, will stand alone. "For whoever wants to save his life will lose it, but whoever loses his life because of Me will find it" (Matthew 16:25).

We've seen that Father has a plan for every one of us who have believed in Him. We've seen that He invites us into closer relationship where He calls us His friends and reveals His will to us. This depends on our passion in knowing and serving Him, our commitment to never quit, and our holy patience to accomplish His will in His time, not ours.

Having daring faith comes from being certain of God's will. We can be certain when it's written in Scripture. In our daily lives, we can be certain when we become His friend and then can hear His voice saying, "This is the way. Walk in it." Getting to this point and then growing stronger in it is a lifetime of passion, perseverance, and patience. It is a relentless pursuit of Him. It is failure and repentance; it is hatred from the very world we yearn to save; it is rejection by those we thought we respected. But in all and through all, never give up. In order to do this, we must learn to love what He loves and hate what He hates. Let's look at that next.

5

CALLED TO HATE SIN

Detest evil.

ROMANS 12:9

Most Christians' knowledge about
God is secondhand information.

ADDISON BEVERE[1]

ON JUNETEENTH WE CELEBRATE THE DAY THE ENSLAVED people of Texas finally learned they were free. They'd been free for over two years, but no one had ever told them. Their masters were content to continue enslaving them until they claimed the truth of President Lincoln's proclamation and threw off the mantle of slavery. Our original master, Satan, is content to let us wallow in the perception that we're still slaves to sin. Now that we're born again, let's throw off the mantle of slavery and start the journey toward holiness, where we'll experience all the joy that our Father has for us.

Jesus said that in order to be His friend we must obey His commands. His commands teach us what He loves and what He hates. What He hates is sin. Nothing in this book is new; these truths have been around since Christ rose from the grave, but they will be new to many people in these modern times. Too many believers today don't understand that they're no longer slaves to sin.

While my family and I were traveling overseas, a friend arranged for a special driver—a Jamaican pastor. He sang hymns and praised Jesus and lamented the traffic under his breath. He was a delight—a fellow sojourner in this life of great joy for those who are abandoned to Jesus.

"There was a lady in Jamaica," he told us in his heavy island accent, "who had a snake . . . a big python. It was her pet. She let it sleep with her. She loved her snake. One day she woke up and the snake was stretched out next to her, from head to toe.

"She was delighted. Her snake wanted to snuggle." He let out a belly laugh. He was so delighted with that line that he repeated it for effect. "Her snake wanted to snuggle her! It only did it that one time until a few months later, when it did it again. And then a few weeks later it did it again. And then only a week later. And then every night . . . that snake would lie beside her every night.

"This lady, you know, she started thinking maybe this was not right. Every morning she woke up to this snake stretched out next to her, its face by her face, its tail by her feet. So she went to a man who knew about snakes. She told him about her snuggly snake." He laughed; that line still killed him.

"You know what he told her, Mr. Ken?" he asked me. He didn't wait for the answer. "That's what a snake does before it eats its prey. It measures itself to see if it can fit the whole body. Her snake was growing and was stretching out more often because it was getting close to eating her. That's what sin is like, Mr. Ken. We think it's harmless. We want to snuggle it. Sin stretches out next to us until it's big enough to swallow us, and then we are enslaved by it forever. We don't exist anymore; we are the sin."

GOD IS HOLY

If you have placed your faith in Christ, you are no longer enslaved to sin. As a member of the Christian community, you've probably heard a statement so often it's become cliché: God is love. I'll bet you've heard that more times than you can remember. The Bible says that in only one place—1 John 4:8; however, the Bible says God is holy countless times.

We are never told to be love as God is love, but we are told to be holy as He is holy (Leviticus 11:44–45, 19:2, 20:7; 1 Peter 1:16). How often do you hear people say that God is holy? Why do we emphasize God's love but not His holiness? Both are true, but repetition in the Bible brings emphasis. We're told that God is not just holy but "Holy, holy, holy," which signifies extreme emphasis (Isaiah 6:3; Revelation 4:8).

As a culture, we're comfortable with His love but not His holiness. If we're comfortable only with His love and not His holiness, it's because we don't truly understand His love. Too many of us have accepted a lie and see His love in narcissistic terms. We see His love for us while forgetting that He loves our brother and our sister just as much as He loves us.

This is where we see holiness and true love come together. As Jesus said, the law is based on two commandments—to love God and to love others. Paul said, "The entire law is fulfilled in one statement: Love your neighbor as yourself" (Galatians 5:14). We understand that all sin hurts others. In order to truly love others, we must learn to hate what hurts others—sin. How often have we gossiped about fellow saints? Slandered them? Betrayed them? Have we considered, as we did so, that God— who is love—is love for them just as much as He is for us?

Many of those in the church live empty, fruitless lives. They wonder why their prayers aren't answered. They wonder why some saints have blessed lives, happy marriages, and godly kids, while they are miserable.

Sometimes God feels far away. He doesn't feel like a Father. He seems distant, as though He's not even hearing our prayers. When God feels far away, we must remember that He doesn't move—we move. The only ones responsible for this distance are us. It comes from unrepented sin in our lives. It comes when we aren't seeking to be holy as God is holy.

At the beginning of this chapter, my friend Addison Bevere is quoted: "Most Christians' knowledge about God is second-hand information." What he's saying is that too few Christians understand God's Word on their own and depend on the teaching of others. As the teaching of others becomes more corrupted, just as we were promised it would (1 Timothy 4:1; 2 Timothy 4:3), many are falling into the trap of sin because of a mistaught understanding of God's holiness and His hatred of sin. Many Bible teachers today are teaching a false Jesus. The true Jesus and what life in Him means is rarely taught. Instead we're taught about a false idol named Jesus. We're taught of a weak, feckless man who was a really, really nice guy whom the Romans finally killed, and something about that poor guy made it okay for us to do whatever we want and have our sins forgiven because, you know—God is love.

No. Jesus was a mighty King who gave His life for us—it wasn't taken from Him—and He demands that we do the same: we lay down our lives and turn from our sins. When we do, we learn to be holy as He is, and then we can experience true joy and blessing in our lives. As we grow, our attraction to sin diminishes and God promises that He is "enabling you both to desire and to work out His good purpose" (Philippians 2:13). We begin to desire what He wants and are therefore constantly filled with satisfaction because we're always getting what we want—His will.

SIN HAS CONSEQUENCES

If you've placed your faith in Christ, you are forgiven of all the sins you have committed or will commit, but the consequences of those sins remain. If I drive drunk and cause an accident and kill someone, the grace of Jesus covers that sin, and I am still His and will still be with Him when I die. But the person is still dead.

Sin in a believer is like rot. It erodes the soul and clouds the mind. It is impossible to escape its consequences. We must flee from sin in every way. This sounds hard, but like everything else in our walk with Christ, the closer we are to Him, the easier it gets, because He changes our desires and sin loses its allure.

Philippians 2:12–13 says, "Continue to work out your salvation with fear and trembling, for it is God who works in you to will and to act in order to fulfill his good purpose" (NIV). Each of us must work out our salvation, seeking God's will and His assignment for us in this life. As we do, He works inside us to want what He wants and to act out what He wants. Our will becomes the same as His will, and that is why walking out a life abandoned to Christ is so filled with joy—because when your will and His are aligned, life is filled with deep satisfaction.

Sin is the great wall that inhibits us from reaching Him. Do you remember the story in Genesis 4 of Cain killing Abel because of his jealousy? God told Cain that he had a decision to make. He could hold on to anger and bitterness, demanding his own way, or he could listen to God and do what was right.

Cain chose anger. He chose sin and it took possession of him. By choosing anger and sin, he became a slave to it. Cain chose bitterness and blame over God's grace.

The choice presented to Cain is the choice we face every day—multiple times a day. Jesus tells us to make the choice daily to follow Him. Sin is "crouching," the Bible says (Genesis 4:7). It wants to rule us, to control us. Our own way is the path to slavery and death.

Human beings were created to rule the earth, but when we chose sin—rebellion against God—everything changed. Instead of ruling the world, we would now be ruled by it. Sickness, war, decay, suffering, and hatred resulted. Because of Christ's sacrifice we have a choice. We can rule over sin. We can choose God's grace over the demands of our flesh.

It is important to repent daily of any sins of which we're aware, and to ask God to reveal unknown sins in us so we can deal with them. Often sins of pride, slander, gossip, and envy are habits, and we're not even aware of their grip on us. As we grow, we become aware of the terrible effects of sins we didn't even realize we were committing. We bring those to God, and He will always forgive them (1 John 1:9). Sin can become a habit we aren't aware of, but as we draw near to God, His Spirit will point these things out in us to clean us up. A habit is only a habit until we're aware of it, and then it's a choice.

THE REST OF THE STORY

The Jamaican pastor said that we "become the sin" by being devoured by it, like the snake that wanted to eat its owner. I've seen what he means. As a police officer in Los Angeles, I used to take new "boots" (what we called rookies) to a dark section of the city where the worst heroin addicts gathered in their misery. These were the heavily diseased people who congregated to try to stay safe while they got high and awaited death. I wanted new cops to understand the devastation of drugs and how they worked. I'd have the boot watch the addicts, whom we called "hypes," melt the heroin in a spoon and inject it so they'd understand the process and know how to recognize someone who was on heroin. Most could no longer inject in their arms or legs because their veins had collapsed from so many injections. They'd had to find creative ways to use other veins.

I'd gather the other hypes around and interview them for the young boots. They'd share their regrets at starting drugs, heroin in particular, and wish they could go back. Their identities all came from being addicts. They'd all insist there was nothing anyone could do for them. They'd been swallowed by the snake. They'd lost all other sense of identity—they were their addiction, and the end was near for most of them.

But is there scientific proof of this, and does "personal" sin that affects only the one doing it really hurt others? In his book *The Freedom Fight*, a troubling examination of the effects of sin, Ted Shimer points out a study conducted in the 1980s about pornography addiction. Eighty men and eighty women who had never seen pornography were divided into three test groups. The three groups were shown media for five hours a week for six weeks. One watched only porn, one watched half normal media and half porn, the third watched only normal media and was therefore still never exposed to pornography. They were then asked some questions, and the responses show the disturbing effect of even the small amount of pornography to which they were exposed:[2]

Is pornography offensive?

Group with zero exposure—75 percent "Yes"
Group with 5 hours exposure—26 percent "Yes"

What should be the prison sentence for rape? (average response)

Group with zero exposure—12 years
Group with 5 hours exposure—6 years

Do you support the women's rights movement?

Group with zero exposure—71 percent males, 82 percent females "Yes"

Group with 5 hours exposure—25 percent males,
52 percent females "Yes"

Should pornography be restricted from minors?

Group with zero exposure—83 percent "Yes"
Group with 5 hours exposure—36 percent "Yes"

The group that watched half porn and half normal media had results that were between the two extreme groups. These are people who should have the same results. The only difference in their perspective is having viewed pornography. Notice the shocking effect viewing porn for only a short time had on the desire to respect and protect women and children. Sadly (and tellingly), in 2013, the University of Montreal wanted to conduct a similar study but couldn't find enough men who had never viewed pornography.[3]

Even private sin hurts others. It changes our perspectives away from God and His precepts to one in which we align ourselves with His enemy. It is when we've learned to throw off the yoke of sin that we start to become like Jesus, where we're on the road to becoming His friend. Now we can start to become the saint our heart yearns to be. It's then that we can start to become courageous. It's then that we can become like the great saints we've read about, who were daring in a cowardly world.

PART 2

LIVING OUT A DARING FAITH

6

LOSING OURSELVES IN HIM

*My eyes will be on the faithful in the
land, that they may dwell with me.*

PSALM 101:6 NIV

*The greatest in the world is the one who
rules the most. The greatest in the kingdom
of God is the one who serves the most.*

TIM DUNN[1]

WHEN WE CHECKED INTO QUANTICO, VIRGINIA, TO START
Marine Corps Officer Candidate School (OCS), I had no idea
of the misery that was to be the summer of 1986. I'd just gone
on my first plane ride ever, a red-eye trip on Western Airlines
from Portland, Oregon, to Washington, DC, connecting
through Seattle and Kansas City. The thrill didn't last long,
as on the final leg of the trip I was seated in the middle seat in
the last row in the smoking section (they had those back then).
I retched and hacked in the smoke, rubbing my burning eyes.

We landed at Dulles Airport, and I drank in the first fresh
air in hours as we were led onto a bus that said USMC on the
side, to start the summer fun. I looked around happily at all
my fellow Marines. They weren't fellow Marines, of course,
because I wasn't a Marine. I was just a cocky college boy about
to learn how unworthy I was to call myself a Marine.

A drill sergeant stepped onto the bus and yelled, "Welcome
to hell, boys! You all just made the biggest mistake of your lives,
and now you belong to me!" This didn't sound like it was going
to be summer fun.

It wasn't. The first day of physical training (PT) we did
what seemed like an endless number of push-ups, stretches,
chin-ups, sit-ups, and leg lifts. It went on for an hour. I was
cocky enough near the end to be thinking that it was hard
but not that bad. It didn't seem any harder than football or

basketball practice. I was ready to hit the showers after a tough workout when the PT instructor said the words I'll never forget: "Okay, warm-ups are over, time to get to work." Warm-ups? That didn't sound good.

It was not good. Marine Corps OCS isn't like other basic training. It isn't really designed to train; it's designed to determine whether a man has what it takes to be a Marine officer. It's designed to make a man quit—and they were good at getting guys to quit. One platoon started with over fifty men and had only eighteen by the time we graduated.

When "warm-ups" were over, we ran, climbed, raced through obstacle courses, and slogged through mud and sand until some guys started throwing up. Drill sergeants screamed in our faces about how completely worthless we were and why we should just quit. At one point, I was so exhausted that I looked down at my M16 rifle and was wondering who was bleeding all over it. I'd rubbed all the skin off my knuckles and was too far gone to feel it.

Through the first two hours of the obstacle courses, push-ups, sit-ups, and running never stopped. I kept picking things to run to and telling myself I'd quit as soon as I got there: a bridge, a tree, the top of a hill. After the first two hours, we finished (we thought) and lined up in formation. Some guys were retching in the bushes from exhaustion and dehydration. Most of us stood at attention, gasping, relieved it was over.

I was sure I couldn't take another step. I had never been so completely spent and was awash in relief and pride for having survived the first day of PT. Suddenly a drill sergeant yelled at us that it wasn't over. I was absolutely sure there was nothing left to give, that I couldn't take another step, but we weren't even close to finished. We launched into another hour of running as some recruits collapsed, drill sergeants standing over them, screaming.

I struggled after that. The cockiness was gone. Any confidence that I had what it took to be a Marine officer was diminished; now I was simply trying to survive. I didn't take notice of anyone else or contribute in any way until we went on one of our longest "humps." A hump was a long hike through the Virginia mountains at a very fast pace with a sixty-five-pound pack, rifle, and helmet. This one was twenty-two miles. We ended up in a massive storm, pitching our tents in driving rain and digging a ditch around the tents to keep them from flooding. I had a hard time with most of the PT, but for a taller man like me, humps were a break. Pull-ups and running were killers, but with long legs and broad shoulders and a childhood of hiking all over the mountains of Oregon, humps were actually enjoyable.

On the humps, everything was opposite from normal PT. The smaller guys labored to keep up while the bigger men enjoyed the idea that we wouldn't be running for the day. There was a man in my platoon named Welch who was laboring badly. He was only about five foot three, with a thick Boston accent; someone I'd never even bothered to talk to before. He was a pull-up machine who'd run by me during PT like I was a statue. Welch needed help. I knew he'd dropped out of a hump before, because the drill sergeants would put anyone who dropped out on display in the back of a dump truck at each roadway we crossed so we could see who quit.

A candidate was given grace if there was a single PT session they couldn't finish for medical reasons, but if they dropped out of two, for any reason, they were disqualified and sent home. I'd seen Welch in that dump truck before. If he failed now, he was out. As we approached a long hill, he started to lag badly, and candidates were brushing him aside to get ahead in the line. I made my way up to him and grabbed him by the belt buckle. "Grab on to my pack, Welch, and I'll pull you up the hill," I said.

And that's what we did for the remaining fifteen miles or so. Every hill we came to, Welch would hold on to my pack, I'd grab his belt, and I'd pull him up. I didn't think much about it until the next day when my drill sergeant pulled me aside and slammed me into a metal Quonset hut. This was his usual manner of communication. I don't recall his name anymore but will never forget his voice or his thinned-down lips and hostile eyes as he screamed up at me. "I saw what you did yesterday, Harrison. Were you trying to cheat the Marine Corps? Were you trying to help someone cheat his way through a hump?"

By this point in OCS, I was so used to being screamed at that I just waited to hear more reasons why I was worthless. Instead his voice softened just a little. "You're a selfish puke. You only worry about yourself. Yesterday you carried Welch the whole day. He wouldn't have made it without you. You actually thought about your platoon instead of just yourself. You might just have what it takes to be a Marine after all, Harrison. Maybe you're not totally worthless."

I was shocked that he'd said something encouraging in any way. After weeks of being torn down, it was bewildering to have even the semblance of a kind word spoken. He started to walk away as I basked in my new status of not being totally worthless. It was probably the shocked expression on my face that made him turn around. "Someone's always watching, Harrison," he said.

JESUS' BLANK CANVAS

The Marine Corps' goal of basic training is to tear a recruit down and then build him up again. They tear down individuality and any reason a recruit has for pride or arrogance until he begins to despair, and then they have the blank canvas they need to train him to be a Marine. They can't work with individuals who think they bring something special, so they're very effective at retraining a recruit's thinking into an understanding that what he brings is his desire and ability to be a Marine and nothing more.

The greatest enemy of Jesus' church and of each of His children's souls is their pride. It is the idea that we have something to offer outside of being filled and used by the Holy Spirit for God's kingdom purpose that leads to so many broken lives, families, and churches. When we think the coming of God's kingdom has anything to do with our talent, we are filled with panic at failure, which leads to blame, manipulation, and despair. In success it leads to that insidious sin of pride, where we elevate ourselves over our brothers and sisters because we think we're more loved or more valuable.

It's a cliché that Jesus is teaching us something through all our trials. He is—but it's better for us to think, not that we need to learn something, but that we need to *unlearn* something. Most of us, upon receiving Christ as our Savior, think we're bringing something to His family. If we think that we bring hang-ups, prejudices, wounds, bitterness, and addiction, we're right. But some of us are proud of our abilities, and we're happy for Jesus that He gets to have us on His team. We're babies. We've been born again but don't yet realize that we contribute nothing to our salvation but our own depravity. In order to become holy, we must be stripped of our worldly confidence and understand that our only value is in complete dependence on Christ.

When we're born, we're utterly dependent on our mother for life. Everything from our feeding to our health depends on her care. We're unaware of how dependent we are; we simply yield to her. Our problems begin as we grow and become aware of our independence. We enter our "Terrible Twos" and think maybe we will touch that hot stove, or run to the edge of that cliff, or pull on the dog's tail. Slowly, and sometimes painfully, we learn that maybe Mom isn't trying to keep us from the glorious pleasures of the hot stove—maybe she knows a thing or two about what's good for us and what isn't.

Our childhood becomes a long lesson in unlearning what we became aware of when we discovered our freedom of choice. We struggle with the knowledge that Mom knows better than we do, yet picking up the dog poo looks so exhilarating even as she's yelling "No!"

This is true the first time we're born, and it's true when we're born again. It seems as if God is trying to keep us from so many delights because we aren't mature enough to realize it's all dog poo outside of Him. Our desires are immature; they're still worldly. Only by growing in Christ do our desires mature. Then we start to become holy. Only then do we have anything to offer.

THE GREATEST SERMON EVER PREACHED

Matthew 5 through 7 is the great Sermon on the Mount. It is a message from Jesus about how someone who is already a believer becomes holy, not how someone becomes a Christian. This is clear from the beginning of the passage as Jesus withdraws from the crowd and preaches the sermon only to His disciples. The message was meant only for His disciples then, and it is meant only for those who would be His disciples today.

I've heard many people say that it is impossible to live up to the teaching in the Sermon on the Mount, and they're right. It is impossible—without first yielding in faith completely to Jesus' teaching. Without losing oneself in Father's kingdom purpose, which allows the Holy Spirit to have complete control of us, we can never live up to Jesus' statements. This leads us to feel afraid, because Jesus says that if we don't live up to them, we'll be led to "destruction," to "hell" (gehenna—a life pronounced worthless, as we'll see later), or to thinking that He must not mean what He says. But it is possible to live up to them when we are abandoned to Him—and that's His point. Jesus would never demand things from us that are impossible, but He does demand things of us that are possible only if we are completely yielded to Him.

The sermon has become a stumbling block of much of the institutional church because we think Jesus can't be serious, so we skip over the harsh words or seek out teachers or books that will explain to us that He didn't mean what He said and then put a nice spin on it. Our problem comes from the fact that we don't understand who Jesus is and that we've been taught to divide everything into heaven or hell (lake of fire) statements. When we understand that Jesus is offering His disciples a choice, not between heaven or hell—we're already saved—but between a worthless life or a holy life, His statements begin to make sense.

Then we begin to understand the harshness of His words. He is saying that if we lose ourselves in Him by picking up our cross daily (Luke 9:23)—literally making a daily choice to die to our right to ourselves—we can be coheirs with Him and reign with Him forever. Either we can seek comfort and safety in this life on earth, which the Bible calls the equivalent of a blade of grass that springs up in the morning and dies in the noonday sun, or we can lose ourselves in His kingdom purpose and reign with Him for eternity.

So how do we do this? What is the formula? The Sermon on the Mount is the formula. It is the step-by-step process of having God's best in this life and for all of eternity. It is the blessed, harsh, impossible demands He makes on anyone who wants to be called His friend. What Jesus knows as He teaches His exasperated disciples is that it is not only possible but it's easy when we're filled with the Holy Spirit.

Institutional religion is the opposite of Jesus' intent. Religion seeks to clean up the outside through rules and judgment, rather than changing the inside. Trying hard not to sin, by rule-keeping, leads to a life of misery. To have one's heart completely changed by our Father, so much so that our very desires become His desires, is the aim of Jesus' words. Joy results from having our wills molded to His. We don't lose our will; rather, our will is changed so that we happily choose His best.

The Sermon on the Mount is our Lord's recipe for losing ourselves in Him. As long as we hold on to things in our lives that give us a sense of value apart from Him, we can't grow in Him to our full extent. It is in dying to ourselves daily that we find our true value as sons and daughters of the Most High.

THE GREAT PROMISES

A friend once said that he always reads the last chapter of a novel in the bookstore before deciding whether it's worth buying. That's just weird, but it's helpful with the Sermon on the Mount. Let's first look at the conclusion of the Sermon on the Mount. The promises He gives will help us understand the demands He makes at the beginning. Remember as you read this that He is talking only to His disciples and to those who would give all to become His disciples. His promises are only to those who have obeyed to the point of being totally abandoned to Him.

Matthew 6:25–34—You have no control of your life, so stop worrying about it. The Father loves you and will take care of all your needs. Be constantly about your Father's business and He will give you what He knows you need.

Promise—If you seek His kingdom first, everything you need will be provided.

Matthew 7:1–6—Don't worry about what your fellow Christians are getting. That's none of your business. Several other portions of Scripture talk about correcting our brother or sister in sin (James 5:19–20), but we are to do so only in love and humility, hoping to restore them. Anything beyond that is between them and the Father and doesn't involve us.

Promise—The measure you use to judge others will be the measure used to judge you. The more you love people, the more grace you extend to them, thereby receiving more grace to yourself.

Matthew 7:7–12—Once you've learned complete dependence on Father and stopped worrying about whether your brothers and sisters are getting more than you, understand that He wants you to continue seeking Him, never giving up because He delights in giving His children good things. The reason we often don't think we're getting good things is because we haven't learned the first lesson of complete dependence on Him and therefore don't know what's truly good. We're immature; we still want to pick up the dog poo. Father tells us to keep asking, because in doing so we'll come to understand that our requests change as we mature and that what we once thought was good is now undesirable. Our desires continue to grow until they become the same as His desires (Philippians 2:13). At that point, we're always getting what we ask for because our hearts and desires are like His.

Promise—God loves to give gifts to His disciples when they ask.

Matthew 7:13–23—Be very careful to walk the narrow and lonely path of holiness. There will be many false teachers with elaborate theologies designed to pull you away from the relationship with Father. Many scriptures warn us that people will be filled with jealousy of our freedom and joy in Christ, and they'll seek to pull us onto the wide path that leads to destruction. Some will even claim to do miracles. Stay focused and don't let them deceive you! Those people will be exposed at the judgment.

Promise—Many believers grope along the wide

road of ease and compromise with the world. Only disciples abandoned to His will find the narrow road that leads to abundant life.

Matthew 7:24–27—If you are diligent in obeying Christ's words, you'll be unshakable. No matter what life brings, you will stand strong. If you don't, when tragedy comes you will have a massive fall.

Promise—Losing ourselves in His kingdom will make us unshakable no matter what tragedy comes our way.

Jesus remakes His disciples' identities. Just as, to be truly effective, a Marine must no longer see himself as anything other than a Marine, so it is with a disciple of Jesus. As a new (immature) believer, we read the Sermon on the Mount with a sense of despair. *Jesus can't mean what He says*, we think. *This is impossible!* And our initial impression is right—it is impossible. So we must now navigate a fork in the road. One path is wide and one narrow. The wide one is well populated. It's filled with fellow believers who are still worldly. One is narrow. It's the road traveled by few. It is the one Jesus demands we take if we want to experience the power and joy He promises. It's the same road that leads to blessing in this life and great reward in the next.

The Creator of the universe came to earth with a specific set of very difficult demands. He told us that He will do everything we need for our salvation and keep us from perishing (John 3:16–18). When we put our faith in Him, we are born again. Yet He also told us that we must be willing to walk away from everything, even our families and our lives, in order to meet His demands. Clearly these demands are not for salvation or for "not perishing," so they must be for something else.

Jesus has His eyes on the prize for us. He knows the "good works, which God prepared ahead of time so that we should walk in them" (Ephesians 2:10). While we were dead in our sins as unbelievers, we had no ability to enter a relationship with Him. We were controlled by sin and destined to die in condemnation. Now that we're born again and have the ability to live free from sin, the quality of our lives on earth and our place in eternity depend on our level of relationship with Him.

The Sermon on the Mount gives us the prescription for joy and blessing in this life and rank and rewards in eternity. In the next chapter, let's look at our Lord's demands closely so that we can be sons and daughters that He says He is "proud to call His own."

THE REST OF THE STORY

At the beginning of this chapter, we saw that I had to be torn down by the Marine Corps before being rebuilt into a Marine. They had to take the teenage boy and remove the pride and immature misconceptions. The Marines say that pain is just weakness leaving the body. Our Lord is at work removing the pride and spiritual immaturity that inhibit us from being His disciples.

A friend of mine was in a somewhat well-known worship band. Well-known enough to be on constant national tours, but not well-known enough to pay the bills. As he was praying, he was convicted that, with a new child in the house, he needed to be at home helping his wife.

My friend went to his pastor and asked for a job. He was a talented musician, a godly man who knew Scripture well. He taught at many Bible studies—was there something he could do to earn a living at the church? Yes, there was, his pastor told him—he could be the janitor.

My friend took the job with joy. The minorly famous musician was now pushing a mop and emptying the trash, and he was strangely satisfied. He knew he was in God's will but didn't know why. He figured it was just because he now got to be home with his wife and child.

He figured wrong. The pastor approached him six months later and let him know he was retiring. Would my friend take over as the head pastor? My friend was shocked. People saw him vacuuming the pews—how would they accept him as pastor?

"I'd been praying for my replacement so I could retire," came the answer. "I specifically asked the Lord for you to be my replacement but didn't know how that could be with you traveling all over the country with your band. When you came to me for a job, I knew it was an answer to prayer, but I needed to be sure you were ready. You say people won't accept you because they saw you vacuuming the pews? I say that's exactly why they will accept you."

That pastor, a man called by the Lord to train others to be disciples, understood that in order for my friend to be truly effective, he must first be stripped of any source of pride other than the pride of being called a disciple of Jesus Christ. He understood Jesus' words that the first shall be last and the last first. The next chapter will be difficult to read because it contains Jesus' demands with regard to what it takes to be a disciple. As we go through this together, remember that as we yield to Him, His demands become our own desire. They are no longer a chore but a delight when our overwhelming desire in this life is to be like Him. Our old identity is washed away and a new one takes its place—that of His disciple, receiving the fullness of everything He has promised. We begin to live out a daring faith without even being aware of it.

7

BECOMING BLESSED

Look! I am coming quickly, and My reward is with Me to repay each person according to what he has done.
REVELATION 22:12

I was honored with having a few stones, dirt, rotten eggs, and pieces of dead cats thrown at me.
GEORGE WHITEFIELD[1]

DON ANKENBRANDT CHEATED HIS WAY THROUGH Mrs. Ward's tenth-grade class. Don didn't think much about it until he gave his life to Christ in college and went on a prayer retreat. In it he was convicted that he needed to go back to his high school and apologize to his teacher for what he'd done years earlier.

Don was terrified. In the naivete of youth, he was sure that Mrs. Ward could revoke his diploma and have him kicked out of college. So Don made a deal with God. If he saw his former teacher, he'd ask her for her forgiveness. It was a good deal for Don, because he was away at college while she taught school in his hometown. What were the odds he'd run into her? But then Thanksgiving came, and they both ended up in the same bookstore.

Don approached her in fear and obedience. He told her that he'd given his life to Christ and was changed. He asked for her forgiveness for cheating in her class. And then she started to cry.

That very morning, Mrs. Ward, fed up with her life, had challenged God to make Himself real to her. If He'd show Himself to her that day, she'd place her faith in Him, but if not, she'd reject Him forever. So God sent a scared nineteen-year-old kid who led her to Christ in a bookstore.

Don ran into her a year later in another bookstore. She was shopping for another devotional. Her marriage had been transformed, she told him with a face filled with joy. Her entire family had received Christ.

Don told me that story not long after he'd attended her funeral, forty years later. Mrs. Ward had dedicated her life to Christ. The funeral was filled with her family members, all following Christ because a young man had the audacity to obey God.

SERMON ON THE MOUNT

We looked at the end of the Sermon on the Mount in the last chapter so that we could understand the promises that await us if we meet demands in the first part. Let's now take some time to really look at our Lord's words. He's looking for people like Don Ankenbrandt, who are daring enough to obey no matter the cost—and change the course of entire families.

Jesus had separated Himself from the crowds, drawing away to teach only His disciples. They'd left everything behind for Him. He was now telling them the point of it all. They had the idea that Jesus would be king, He would reign from Jerusalem, and they would rule with Him, that all the enemies of Israel and God would be vanquished, and they were right. All of that would happen—just not in their lifetimes. They were about to learn that the glory, honor, and rewards they'd receive would come only after a lifetime of choosing Christ over self, resulting in humiliation, loss, and martyrdom.

Much of what is written about the Sermon on the Mount has over-theologized it. Jesus was preaching to twelve men, most of whom were uneducated. They would have taken what He said at face value. They would never have come up with the long theological sermons meant to change Jesus' simple words. Let's look at His words with the crazy notion that He said exactly what He meant to say.

Throughout His sermon, Jesus talked about a life lived for Him resulting in great reward, or a life lived in sin and complacency resulting in a wasted life and loss at the judgment seat of Christ. Likewise, He didn't talk about salvation in terms of being saved from condemnation; this sermon is the description of what a holy saint looks like. It illustrates the character of a man or woman who will receive the promises in the sermon, earn crowns, reign with Him, and be at the wedding feast of the Lamb in eternity.

There are many comments in the Bible and in this book on "carnal" Christians. Carnal basically means immature.[2] A new believer is carnal in the sense that they're a baby. Mostly, carnal means immature in the way that an adult can be immature, selfish, and self-absorbed. They take more than they give, they don't have a thirst for Scripture, and they have little prayer life. They're easily tossed around by the newest worldly philosophy, and they can't be counted on to stand for truth when the going gets tough. They are controlled by their flesh and ego because they haven't grown to maturity in Jesus Christ. The master doesn't "know" them, as we see later in chapter 12, "Let's Get Married!" The Sermon on the Mount is the great separator of the carnal believer from the holy believer.

BEATITUDES (MATTHEW 5:3-11)

These are in order of the growth of a Christian into a sanctified, holy believer, who will receive all the inheritance, gifts, crowns, and rulership promised from God. Becoming a disciple is a process. The moment we put our faith in Christ, we become alive. Now we must grow. The Beatitudes are signposts along the way of us becoming the kind of believers Jesus calls friends.

"Blessed are the poor in spirit, for theirs is the kingdom of heaven" (v. 3 NIV).

Most Christians aren't even close to the first Beatitude. They believe in Jesus but have no idea of the level of their depravity or the immense grace and love of the Creator to rescue them. It is growth in Christ that results in becoming poor in Spirit, the realization that I am responsible for the terrible suffering of my Lord, and I contribute nothing to Him. The only thing I can offer is to grow constantly in a love and relationship with Him that is wholly inadequate on my part. But like a parent who loves a little child even though their love can never be returned at the same level from the child, so it is with us and our Father. Pride in a believer is always a sign that they aren't even at this first step yet. This was my thirty-year-old self lying in a hospital bed, terrified to see Christ face-to-face.

"Blessed are those who mourn, for they will be comforted" (v. 4 NIV).

The poorness of spirit grows into mourning. Mourning for the world, for those we see and know, mourning over the horrid consequences of sin. We become more aware of the pain and suffering in the world and mourn that we can't do more to rescue people from sin's clutches. We see violent people, gossips, liars, the sexually perverse, the bitter and hateful—not in anger or indignation, but in a sense of mourning for them, knowing they don't have to be that way if they'd give their lives to Christ. Those who mourn are blessed because they are learning to see sin in its ugliness. They are no longer titillated by its attraction but are repulsed by it. Pornography is repugnant; their reaction is to cover up the girl in the video and tell her about Jesus. Their response to gossip is a heart-wrenching need to pray for the person gossiped about. Sin has lost its shine. They begin to see the world through God's eyes, and they mourn for its state. God will comfort them. He gave all and He has a plan, even if we can't yet understand it all.

"Blessed are the meek, for they will inherit the earth" (v. 5 NIV).

Mourning for the lost and the state of the world shows our heart is becoming like God's. This leads to a growing humility and meekness as gratitude for the sacrifice of Jesus becomes more and more evident. We are learning to see others as more important than ourselves (Philippians 2:3). We don't see them as more valuable—we see all people everywhere as our equals, no one above us and no one beneath us—but we see serving them as more important so that we can encourage them in their walk with God.

"Blessed are those who hunger and thirst for righteousness, for they will be filled" (v. 6 NIV).

Then comes a thirst for righteousness. Knowing God and understanding His will becomes a need like a deep thirst. All other things begin to fade in importance. Like a teenager who suddenly realizes the wisdom of her parents, the believer begins to understand the boundless joy in knowing Father and begins seeking to be on her knees in prayer and deeply studying Scripture. It isn't a chore, it's a need; it isn't devotions, it's love. As a runner yearns to run and a writer must write, a person becoming sanctified needs to be with Father, even while the carnal believers can't understand. She now begins to separate from average believers. They don't understand her anymore. She's becoming a fanatic in their eyes. Even at church, she gets excluded from some groups because she's always wanting to stop and pray and bothering everyone about helping others. But everyone comes to her when they're in trouble. She's their first call when they're in distress, asking if she'd pray for them—and she does. She's becoming holy. She is becoming a daughter with whom Jesus can have growing intimacy.

"Blessed are the merciful, for they will be shown mercy" (v. 7 NIV).

Empathy grows within the saint. No longer is there judgment of those trapped in sin, but rather love and desire to rescue them from its clutches. Righteous indignation turns to a desire to serve. The saint who has become merciful serves not because he has to or because it makes him feel good; the saint serves because he's learned to value the souls of others and will do all to rescue them from sin. He has become like young Don Ankenbrandt, who didn't think losing his diploma too great a price to pay for Mrs. Ward's soul.

My friend Robert Mason, who is white and a successful developer, told me of driving down a street in Atlanta and seeing a Black woman holding a sign that read, "Trans Black lives matter." He pulled his car over. I asked Robert to put his story in writing. Here is what he said:

> With tears in my eyes I realized what a terrible "stand-in" for Jesus I was, but I did the simplest thing I could. I reached into my wallet, pulled out a twenty-dollar bill, looked this person in the eye, and told them, "I want you to know something. You have probably been around a lot of Christians and have probably heard a lot of condemnation, but I want you to know this—Jesus LOVES you! He isn't like so many of His followers (and you would love Him). Please know He *loves* you!"

She started to cry and thanked me. I realized how far off I am from following Christ because this was so rare an experience for me.

As I drove off, I teared up as I thanked God for putting her in my path and helping me clearly see just what Jesus might indeed do in our present circumstances. I prayed that she might come to know Him and I prayed that I might change and become more like my Savior who wasn't ashamed to call me (a wretched, self-righteous sinner) His friend.[3]

Robert didn't see someone differently by race or identity, he didn't see a sinner; he saw someone who needed to be loved. Robert will be shown mercy in his time of need because he showed mercy.

"Blessed are the pure in heart, for they will see God" (v. 8 NIV).

Purity of heart follows. The saint's heart is becoming like God's heart. Ego is almost nonexistent. The saint no longer gets caught up in pride. They don't care who gets credit anymore; their eyes are on Father and on the reward of knowing Him. They let the others have the title or speak in front of big crowds; they only want to listen to the sweet, soft voice of the Holy Spirit and follow where He leads. It may be on the stage, but it's more likely in the gutter where the needy are, or in their closet, praying for others—and there are no crowds to cheer them on.

"Blessed are those who are persecuted because of righteousness, for theirs is the kingdom of heaven. Blessed are you when people insult you, persecute you and falsely say all kinds of evil against you because of me. Rejoice and be glad, because great is your reward in heaven" (vv. 10–12 NIV).

Let's jump ahead a verse here because we're going to come back to the saint becoming a peacemaker. The saint is now experiencing persecution. They're having evil things said about them. People will gossip and lie. Their old friends will fall away; they'll be excluded from the clubs and gatherings. The main persecutors will be their fellow Christians. The carnal believers become offended at such a person. Who does she think she is? The typical Christian doesn't want to be confronted on sins; even if the saint never says a word, her life is conviction enough. It becomes harder to find friends as she becomes aware of how shallow most people are. She had started to see these things as she grew but now they are on full display, as even fellow Christians hate her. When a person's longing is for Father, His Word, and obedience to Him, it becomes difficult to find others on the same path. Rejoice when you've gotten to this point, for Jesus says, "Great is your reward in heaven."

"Blessed are the peacemakers, for they will be called children of God" (v. 9 NIV).

Let's now go back a verse to the last stop before we're promised persecution. Let's spend some time here because this is one of the most misinterpreted verses in the Bible. Many justify passivity and use this and other passages we'll look at to justify inaction in the face of injustice.

Notice Jesus blesses the peacemakers, not the peacekeepers. Making peace requires action and, paradoxically, sometimes involves violence. Peacemakers sometimes use force when it's needed to defend the innocent. My friend General Jerry Boykin of Delta Force killed twenty-eight terrorists in a rescue mission for several missionaries who had been kidnapped. Jerry's attack was so fierce and sudden that not a single missionary was hurt. Jerry, a great man of God, was a peacemaker.

On this subject, let's cover another grossly misunderstood portion of the Sermon on the Mount. Let's jump ahead to verse 39, where Jesus said, "If anyone slaps you on the right cheek, turn to them the other cheek also" (NIV). Turn the other cheek is about as common a cliché as there is in our culture, but what does Jesus mean? Many understand it to say that violence is always wrong. But Jesus isn't talking about violence. A long portion of His talk here is about fleeing immorality and pride.

Did you notice the word in our Lord's quote above that we always leave out? He said, "slaps you on the right cheek." Why would He say "right cheek"? What difference does the cheek make? A lot. All men in the ancient world were right-handed, because they were trained for combat to line up in rows holding their shield in their left hand to defend the man next to them, and their sword in their right.[4]

When a right-handed person throws a punch, they'll strike on the left cheek. To strike on the right cheek is a backhand.

It's how one would've struck a slave or child—someone culturally beneath them. It was a strike of humiliation, not a strike designed for full force. You can see how this now fits into Jesus' context on pride. Many godly people are misled by a poor understanding of this passage into passivity in the face of evil. Jesus is not saying we shouldn't fight back when attacked—He is saying we should never fight back from a place of pride.

Sometimes choosing not to fight back is the greater thing, such as in the story of Jim Elliot, who chose not to fire his rifle as the natives in the Ecuador jungle rushed him with spears and killed him. He gave his life for them, and they eventually became Christians when Jim's wife, Elisabeth, returned years later and shared the gospel with the men who had murdered her husband. But when it comes to oppression, sometimes fighting is the greater thing. Sometimes not fighting back allows wickedness and oppression of the weak to grow. It is the godly saint, living in complete obedience to Father, with no pride involved, who knows the difference.

THE REST OF THE STORY

It may have seemed odd to start this chapter with the simple story of Don Ankenbrandt, but don't let its simplicity pass you by. As we read a chapter like this one, we sometimes have in our head a vision of the great saints. We picture Hudson Taylor and George Müller and Mother Teresa. We think of a goal reachable only by some sort of celebrity Christian, not a nineteen-year-old kid naive enough to think his former teacher could take away his diploma. Jesus said that He wants followers who are like children, obeying even though they can't see the big picture or how they fit in. God is not looking for the greatest speakers or leaders, He isn't looking for the physically gifted or good-looking, He isn't looking for the high and mighty. He's looking for those with the audacity to obey even though they can't see the way forward. What does that look like?

If your daughter were stuck in a well, would you ever give up? Would you not endure to your own death to free her? Would you not sacrifice all pride, screaming out for help to anyone, even your worst enemy? Or strip off your clothes and throw them down to her to keep her warm, even while you suffered naked and cold? Why would you do all those things? Love. Yet Jesus calls us to love Him more than we love our own daughter (Matthew 10:37). We would sacrifice all, persevere through all, humiliate ourselves beyond any semblance of pride to save our daughter. Jesus demands that we love Him more than that. And how do we love Him? By keeping His commandments.

Am I willing to give all to know Him? Jesus said anyone who doesn't say goodbye to all his possessions isn't worthy of Him. This doesn't mean giving them all away. He gave them to you to steward. It means regarding everything—your money, possessions, health, reputation, spouse, and children—as His. You will give all to know Him. It's in our nature to desire to be as close to Father as we can, but our sinful nature pulls us in the other direction. God's Word gives us the formula for ultimate intimacy with Him. At the same time, He warns us to count the cost: Do we really want to know Him badly enough to pay the price (Luke 14:26–35)?

We saw in chapter 3 that James Robison is a friend of Jesus. James is in a long line of saints—friends of Jesus—who never gave up and never relented. The foundation for us comes from the very beginning of the church. As John sat on Patmos, exiled there by the Romans because they were unable to kill him, he must have been thinking of his fellow apostles. They'd been sawn in two, crucified, beheaded, skinned alive, stoned, and beaten to death. John alone survived.

It wasn't just the apostles who gave all. John had seen his fellow leaders, like Luke and Mark, killed as well. John had watched men and women burned to death and thrown to wild animals under the rule of Nero for the entertainment of the masses. They had one thing in common. None relented. These were Jesus' friends. These were the people who gave all, and their faith resulted in eternal rewards and privileges for eternity.

God hasn't left us unaware. He promises great joy and eternal rewards for those whom He calls friends. He promises us that the sacrifices we make in this temporary life will be compensated more than we can know.

STAYING SALTY

You are the salt of the earth. But if the salt should lose its taste, how can it be made salty? It's no longer good for anything but to be thrown out and trampled on by men.
MATTHEW 5:13

God didn't leave us on this earth to make it a better place to go to hell from.
DR. RALPH "YANKEE" ARNOLD[1]

WHEN I PLAYED SMALL COLLEGE BASKETBALL, WE HAD A player on the team named Tony who rarely got on the court during games. He was a phenomenal athlete. He could do 360-degree dunks, he was smooth as silk, and he could hit three-point shots from anywhere on the court. His problem was that he refused to play defense. Our team's personality was intense defense and relentless hustle and effort. This great athlete put out effort only when he had the ball, and then it was electric.

There was another player on the team, Dave, who wasn't a good athlete, but he was the star. He almost never came off the court. He wasn't smooth and he couldn't shoot from beyond ten feet, but he had a motor that never stopped. He played stifling defense and dove onto the floor for every loose ball, screened out for every rebound, and played with relentless dedication to fundamentals.

Tony played only for the cheers of the crowd. He played the brand of basketball that he wanted that got him the most glory in his own mind. On the few occasions he got on the court when we were up by a large margin near the end of the game, he would usually find a way to have some thundering tomahawk dunk that got the crowd on their feet. Dave got almost no cheers. Diving for loose balls and playing strong defense doesn't make the crowd erupt—but he was the reason we won games.

The differences in the two players were their goals and their audience. The first player's goal was his own glory, and his audience was the crowd. The second player's goal was only winning, and he had an audience of one—his coach. The fans would ask me all the time why Tony didn't play more. He seemed so "awesome," they'd say. But though he appeased the crowds, he added no real value to the team or to winning. At the end of the season, Dave was MVP of the team and voted All Conference by the coaches he'd played against. The crowds couldn't recognize who had value, but the coaches and other players did.

This simple illustration gets us to the core of our Lord's sermon. What is your goal and who is your audience? The crowds of Christians on the wide road, and even the people of the world, will cheer you when you do the things they approve of—things that have the appearance of value. But the truly holy, those on the narrow road, know one another.

We've seen Jesus describe what holiness looks like and the promises that come from Him if we do the hard work of becoming holy. He tells us that we should be like salt and light. With no refrigeration in Jesus' day, salt was used to preserve meat and kill the bad bacteria on it. As salt, we need to remove evil where we see it; as light, we need to expose it where we see it, shining our light on the good news of Jesus. Jesus said that if we aren't active, we aren't worth anything to His kingdom, worthy only of being "thrown out" (Matthew 5:13).

We must always remember that He is the loving Father in the parable of the prodigal son (Luke 15:11–32), waiting patiently for us to repent of our inaction and sin, who will run to us the moment we do. If you've been lazy, if you've been like tasteless salt, confess your sins and change today. He will immediately restore you (1 John 1:9). It's time to get back in the battle.

A MOTLEY CREW

As we read of Jesus telling the disciples that He is the fulfillment of the law, it's helpful to remember the preconceived notions most people in Israel had of the coming Messiah. The people had held tightly to the prophecies of Messiah coming as King and Conqueror, and they'd adapted the prophecies to their current situation—sure that He would conquer the oppressive Romans. The people had closed their eyes to Isaiah 53, which promised that Messiah would be scorned and killed.

Even so, certainly Messiah wouldn't come from a nondescript region like Nazareth with a bunch of uneducated fishermen, a terrorist, and a tax collector. Nor would he look like Jesus. As a carpenter, Jesus spent the first thirty years of His life primarily as a stonemason.[2] Carrying, chiseling, and building with rock would have made Him thick with muscle, His hands rough and strong. He wasn't the scrawny, malnourished character we see in so many movies.

His disciples were similar. Fishermen in those days spent their lives hauling heavy nets up and down all day. They had broad backs and shoulders and were used to fighting off other boats when they got into a school of fish and the others started homing in. These men weren't fishing for fun; their catch that day determined how their families would eat that week or whether their wives got something nice. It was rough business for rough men. Everything about them, from their clothing to their accents to their demeanor, revealed who they were. Peter, James, and John, Jesus' top three disciples, seemed to always be itching for a fight. Of course they were—this was all they knew.

One of the disciples, Simon the Zealot, was a terrorist. The Zealot party trained in creating riots and slipping thin knives between the armor of Roman soldiers. But the worst was Matthew. Tax collectors weren't just greedy traitors. They were organized-crime bosses. They purchased a tax region from the Romans. Rome dictated the amount of taxes it expected from that region, and the tax collector kept the rest. His level of wealth came from how effectively he could take money from his countrymen, who had no idea what the actual taxes were, only what the collector told them. They closed off city gates, set up roadblocks, and had spies in the markets to take money from anyone they could. This often involved hiring thugs. They were the most loathed creatures in Israel.

As Jesus gathered His band of muscular ruffians to teach them about holiness, it must've been a strange sight. Jesus certainly didn't look like royalty. "He didn't have an impressive form or majesty that we should look at Him, no appearance that we should desire Him" (Isaiah 53:2). Israel's idea of a king was like their first king, Saul, who was tall and handsome, not

Jesus, who was a rough blue-collar man with unimpressive looks.

Imagine the average person seeing this band of men, trying to grasp Jesus' claims to be Messiah, thinking that if He doesn't seem like a king, maybe He's more of a revolutionary. That certainly must have been what His group looked like. Then He started talking about love and sacrifice, dying to the rights to oneself, being meek and poor in spirit. The confusion and doubt of the Israelites can certainly be understood. And then He healed a blind man or raised someone from the dead and a person was left to decide whether they'll walk away from every prejudice and conviction they've ever known and follow Him, or turn away back to the life they understand. Jesus is asking us all the same question today.

HOLINESS THAT SURPASSES THE PHARISEES'

Jesus said He is the fulfillment of the law. This is no small thing. He took the oppressive yoke of the law upon Himself—we no longer need to keep it. Then He laid down a huge bombshell: if a person wants to get into the kingdom of heaven, they must have righteousness that "surpasses that of the scribes and Pharisees" (Matthew 5:20). Isn't this impossible?

Yes, it is. That is to say, it is impossible to surpass the righteousness that they present themselves to have, which is completely exterior. Holiness is being set apart to God, and this comes from the inside. It starts at the core because the only audience is God, who sees into the depths of our souls. Religion seeks to clean up the outside, even if the inside is rotten, because its audience is the world.

Religion is the outward appearance of righteousness, while holiness is true righteousness that comes from within. When I was on the LAPD, I trained very hard to be in shape. I lifted weights, ran, and trained in combat. The reason was that my life, my partner's life, and the general public's lives depended on it. Studies have shown that the better shape a police officer is in, the less likely a bad guy is to attack them or resist arrest. I didn't lift weights and train so hard to have nice muscles, though that was a benefit that came from it; I trained to be as strong and fit as possible to withstand attacks when they came.

We had gyms at every police station, and I'd usually be there two hours before roll call to work out. There was another officer in my division whom I saw there sporadically. He had a big chest and arms, but his build seemed strangely bloated. One day he showed up to lift with me and I was surprised how weak he was for all the bulk of his muscles. It turned out he didn't really want to lift—he wanted to get marriage advice. As we were talking, he let me know he was cycling on steroids and was an alcoholic. His muscles were for appearance only; they didn't come from his core and therefore had little strength. They were for show for the world but had no value for withstanding attacks from evil men. So it is with religious people compared to holy people. In the day of testing, they have only soft, showy works designed for people to see instead of a strong spiritual core.

Bearing this in mind, we see Jesus launch into another very misunderstood portion of Scripture. He was explaining what true holiness is, not religion. Jesus said that if we're angry with our brother or look at a woman with lust, we're in danger of hell (Matthew 5:21–30). Jesus was talking about the condition of our hearts and what holiness looks like in our everyday lives and thoughts.

I've heard numerous Christians discuss what lust is and how long a man can look at a woman before being guilty. I've been to men's conferences and sadly heard teachers say that to look once is fine but twice is a sin. They wring their hands in false guilt in a legalistic and pharisaical reading of our Lord's words. Worse, it has made many Christians and Christian institutions behave in shameful ways toward women because of their false guilt, blaming women for their "lust."

It's common for people to misunderstand this passage, thinking it means the opposite of what Jesus intended. In fact, Jesus was talking about holiness in the face of daily temptations. He was talking about not letting our light go out or our salt lose its taste.

Lusting for a woman is not in thinking she's attractive, but whether you'd commit adultery with her if you could. If no one was looking, if there was no way to get caught, if God wasn't watching, what would you do? A holy person is a content person. When a person is poor in spirit, mourning for the world, merciful, pure, hungering for righteousness, they aren't spending time wishing they could have an affair with their neighbor's wife. A man can acknowledge that she's beautiful and also see a soul who needs Jesus or who needs to be helped to grow in Jesus just like anyone else. A holy man is filled with gratitude for the wife God gave him or is waiting patiently for the day He brings him one. He doesn't want anyone else's wife.

People who try hard not to lust are missing the entire point. They haven't reached the very first portion of the Sermon on the Mount. They haven't become poor in spirit and cast their cares upon the Lord, who will fill them with His presence. He'll start them on the narrow road when they've finally given up trying to get on it in their own righteousness.

THROWN INTO HELL

A last note on this—when Jesus said one is in danger of being thrown into hell, He is not referring to the lake of fire. We often confuse the two places as the same, and they are not the same. The word for hell here refers to Gehenna, or the Valley of Hinnom. In ancient Israel, the bodies of the Israelites' enemies and of people who made no impact were burned in the valley so they wouldn't take up space in a grave.[3] To be burned there was a pronouncement of a life that didn't matter. Jesus was not saying that if a person commits adultery or murder he will go to hell. David wrote scripture after his affair with Bathsheba and the murder of her husband, Uriah. He is most certainly in heaven. Jesus meant that to allow such sins into your heart can cause you to lose your saltiness and risk having your life pronounced at the judgment as having had no value in the kingdom of heaven.

RELATIONSHIP

Jesus moved through the other portions of the sermon: honoring marriage, honoring one's word, not retaliating in pride, loving enemies, giving quietly, praying privately, not worrying, asking for things, and not judging. These are all instructions of a Father to His children. The people of Israel had become "religious" and lost what it meant to be in love with God. They'd come up with slick workarounds to justify divorce or make promises they knew they'd break. They weren't honoring God's heart; they were making rules that would appease one another. His instructions are the practical words to His kids. He told them to stop playing games that placate others when it comes to holiness. Either you give all for Him or you don't, and He is the only judge.

These are the aspects of faith and humility that He honors: honoring His children, honoring Him by not using our relationship with Him to curry favor with others (look how generous and religious I am!), and trusting Him to provide and do what's right by us.

Jesus was giving the disciples a model for how they could go from being "slaves" of God to children and friends of God—to having the kind of intimacy where He can trust them with His plans, as we saw earlier. In the sermon we're given two primary concepts. The first is from Matthew 5:19, where He tells us that some people will be least in the kingdom of heaven, and some will be greatest. The second is that on several occasions Jesus referred to rewarding those who live by His sermon. This starts a theme throughout the New Testament—God rewarding those who live up to the concepts of the Sermon on the Mount.

PERSEVERING FOR A LIFETIME

I mentioned earlier doing a lot of physical training. In college I was hired as a trainer at a gym. A pattern emerged with many of the people who came to get trained, which seemed to repeat itself. They usually lasted about two months. They'd start off with a bang, going through the initial stages of soreness. They'd see minor results and start to look down on those who weren't working out diligently like they were. Then the first excuse would come on why they needed to miss a workout—they had class, they had a cold, or they had a flat tire. After that, in almost every case, there would be a couple more excuses and then they'd never show up again.

Sadly I've seen the same pattern with most people I've discipled in Christ. I was leading a Bible study several years ago that took off. It was very well attended, and we had people who would call in from all over the country, from Oregon to Virginia. When we completed the study, I announced that it would now turn into a prayer group. The hour and a half we'd spent studying and sharing stories would now be spent in prayer for one another, our families, our churches, and our country. I challenged them that, based on my experience, two-thirds of the attendees would fall out within two months. "Prayer is hard," I told them. "Many people want to be diligent in prayer for others for a brief time, but few have the perseverance."

Most people disagreed or took issue with that, assuring that they'd be around for the duration, but eight weeks later someone pointed out that we had exactly one-third of the original people.

My wife, Elliette, and I have led several prayer groups. We've found that many couples show up excited, expressing joy that they've finally found a group of Christians committed to praying, but rarely do they last long. Our house is a revolving door of those who show up in need, distraught over their job, marriage, kids, the state of the world . . . but very few continue after a few months. We found that we had to limit the time for prayer requests at the beginning as it inevitably turned into a time for conversation instead of praying. We've had many people who, after showing up a few times, simply started to text their list of prayer requests but never showed up again.

Those who last beyond a few months are usually there for the long term. Many people get excited when they hear the things of God or read a book or hear a great sermon, but few endure. Religiously cleaning up the outside for a while isn't so hard, but becoming holy, changing from the inside, and giving God's Spirit more room to grow is a lifetime of work with perseverance.

To be bold in a moment isn't easy, but to have daring faith is nearly impossible. It will not come in a flash. It is a lifetime of dying to yourself daily, failing, repenting—but never quitting.

THE REST OF THE STORY

Our basketball team was competing for a spot in the playoffs while Tony watched from the bench. We were down by three points with less than a minute to go in the game. The other team had the ball and was running out the clock. They were spread out and passing the ball around, when suddenly Dave erupted from under the basket and stole the ball near midcourt by a fingertip. The slowest guy on the court drove down and thundered a dunk over three players, getting fouled and tying the game.

The crowd erupted in shock. No one even knew Dave could dunk. Dave never had a reason to until that moment. His film study, hard work, and relentless drive to win had prepared him for the moment where, when his team needed him the most, he was ready to make a play that seemed beyond his ability.

When the moment of testing comes, who you are will all come rushing forward in that instant. Jesus says die to yourself daily. Live out holiness in the moment. Don't worry whether you'll have what it takes tomorrow, for "tomorrow will worry about itself" (Matthew 6:34). Jesus invites each of us into deeper and deeper relationship with Him, along with all the sorrow, pain, joy, and rewards that come with it. He is not inviting us to follow someone's rules or religion; He is not inviting us to appease the crowd along the wide road; He invites us into the holy living of the few along the narrow road.

PART 3

REWARDS FOR A
DARING FAITH

9

YOUR NAME IN THE BOOK OF LIFE

Then I saw a great white throne and One seated on it.
Earth and heaven fled from His presence, and no place
was found for them. I also saw the dead, the great and
the small, standing before the throne, and books were
opened. Another book was opened, which is the book of
life, and the dead were judged according to their works by
what was written in the books. . . . And anyone not found
written in the book of life was thrown into the lake of fire.
REVELATION 20:11–12, 15

If I am devoted solely to the cause of humanity,
I will soon be exhausted and come to the
point where my love will waver and stumble.
But if I love Jesus Christ personally and
passionately, I can serve humanity, even
though people treat me like a "doormat."
OSWALD CHAMBERS[1]

I WAS ON A HUNTING TRIP WITH ABOUT TWENTY MEN WHO were business and political leaders. I had been invited to provide some spiritual leadership and to witness to some of the men if opportunity arose. About half the men were Christians and the other half not. As we sat around a large dinner table in the lodge, the issue of politics and then religion came up. One of the men stood and gave an arrogant and loud diatribe about how Muslims and Christians both believe in Jesus and therefore worship the same god.

We politely listened, and when he was done, I responded, calmly giving a ten-minute synopsis of the gospel. I listed Jesus' claims to being God and His grace to all people everywhere. I included the necessity to believe in Him and who He was, to activate that grace. I quoted John 3:18: "Anyone who believes in Him is not condemned, but anyone who does not believe is already condemned, because he has not believed in the name of the One and Only Son of God."

I pointed out that Christianity and Islam both believe in someone called Jesus. Christians believe who He was and claimed to be, which is the Son of God, one with the Father. Muslims deny who He claims to be; therefore, they don't believe in Him. As an example, if you and I both say we believe in George Washington, and you say he was the first president of the United States while I insist that, no, he's just a guy who owns a deli on Forty-Second Street, we may both believe in a man named George Washington, but we most certainly don't believe in the same man.

I concluded by saying that anyone who places their faith in Jesus, the Son of God, who gave His life for our sins, is saved from their sins and from the penalty of eternal damnation in the lake of fire. Anyone who denies His identity and His sacrifice denies Him and will perish in their sins.

Most of the Christians there were grateful for the gospel presentation, and privately said as much throughout the evening. The next morning, before the sun rose, one of the other Christians wanted to correct me on talking about "hell." It was inappropriate to discuss punishment, he said. A person should talk only about the positive, never the negative. When I asked him about the fact that Jesus talked about hell quite often, more so than heaven, he had no answer.

"I just tell people that if they accept Jesus, they can be like me," he said.

"You're a self-made billionaire," I answered him. "You're a powerful public figure, who is known and respected. Is it realistic to say they can be like you?"

"I just don't like talking about the negative" was his only answer.

I have great respect for my friend and think many people who follow Christ believe as he does. But we do a disservice by not giving the whole truth. There is indeed some significant negatives that Jesus was clear about, for those who reject Him.

We should do all we can, in gentleness and grace, to give the whole gospel to all who will listen, but also the bad news for those who reject the truth.

THE BOOK OF LIFE

Those whose names are written in the Book of Life will be at the judgment seat of Christ, also called the bema seat. This bema seat is only for the children of God, the believers. It is a judgment of rewards for a job well done, a place for granting privileges, titles, and crowns.

Those whose names are not in the Book of Life will be at a different judgment seat, called the great white throne. It is a judgment of condemnation. Everyone who is brought before this throne is there only to find out the extent of their punishment. They will all be separated from the love of the Creator forever. They will all spend eternity in the lake of fire, though Scripture seems to indicate that parts of it are worse than others, since their condemnation is also determined by other books, in addition to the Book of Life, and based on their works (Revelation 20:11–15).

THE SINS OF CONDEMNATION

"But the cowards, unbelievers, vile, murderers, sexually immoral, sorcerers, idolaters, and all liars—their share will be in the lake that burns with fire and sulfur, which is the second death" (Revelation 21:8).

If you're reading this and wondering whether your name is written in the Book of Life, it's first helpful to look at how you know it isn't. As we discussed earlier, Revelation 21:8 gives a list of eight sins. If a person's life is typified by them, he will have a share in the lake of fire. Since salvation (being rescued from the lake of fire) comes from grace alone and not by works, this verse is saying that anyone whose life is typified by these sins never believed in Jesus.

It isn't saying anyone who has committed these sins cannot be saved; it is saying those who unrepentantly have a lifestyle of them are not saved. God's grace is sufficient to cover every sin. David's affair with Bathsheba and the murder of her husband is well-known to anyone who has read their Bible, and their son Solomon had a thousand wives, most of whom worshiped foreign gods (idolatry). Yet both kings, guilty of adultery, murder, and idolatry, wrote Scripture. Simon, in Acts 8:9–24, practiced sorcery but was pronounced a believer and baptized. Aaron, the first priest, practiced idolatry when he worshiped the golden calf. All these people are clearly in heaven.

So what is a "liar"? What is the "sexually immoral"? It is appropriate for us to examine ourselves to ensure we are walking in the faith and are truly children of God (2 Corinthians 13:5; 2 Peter 1:10). Everyone whose name is written in the Book of Life has the Holy Spirit's indwelling and therefore can't commit these eight sins without being convicted by the Holy Spirit.

Believers, upon committing such sins, are convicted and

repent; unbelievers insist this is how God created them, shrug their shoulders, or feel bad but don't truly repent. A believer is convicted even when she's the only one who knows of the sin, because her heart breaks at offending her Father in heaven. The unbeliever is primarily concerned about whether someone knows what he did.

This passage reiterates what we saw earlier, that people tend to become their sin. God judges people by giving them what they want. As they persist in their sin, He turns them over to a corrupted mind (Romans 1:26–31). They simply get all they want of it without God to convict them. Those who unrepentantly commit cowardly acts enough times become cowards; those who commit sexual perversion long enough without repenting simply become perverts.

When they insist that this is who they are, they're right. They try to justify their sin by saying, "God made me this way." God didn't make them that way, sin did, and they chose sin over God. Believers walking in sin are never abandoned by God and never stop being convicted of their wrongdoing. So, confident in God's boundless grace and His promise to wipe away all sins from the one who believes, let's examine our hearts together to ensure our names are written in the Book of Life.

GRACE AFTER DEATH

When it comes to death, there are essentially three macro-categories of people: unbelievers; carnal Christians (those on the wide road of ease and comfort who will weep and gnash their teeth at wasted lives); and sanctified, holy believers who have given all (those on the narrow road who will reign with Christ). The individual resurrection of each believer will differ in glory, and unbelievers will be judged by what is written in the books of their lives. We'll look at this in detail in the next few chapters.

God's grace can cover all, but it doesn't. He has put a condition on His grace. By His decree the King has said that His grace covers those who believe in Him and it doesn't cover those who reject Him (John 3:18). If you wonder, what about those who never heard of Him, who couldn't accept or reject, His answer is that all are accountable because God has made His nature plain to all (Romans 1:19–20). Does this mean people can come to saving knowledge with no one to tell them the good news? It sounds like it, though Paul asked in the same book (in Romans 10:14) how they can hear without a preacher. We don't know how this works exactly, but we know Jesus told us to go to the ends of the earth to make disciples for Him, telling the good news of His love to those who don't know and helping those who do to become holy sons and daughters.

The eight sins of condemnation are not for those who have confessed their sins and believe in the Lord Jesus as their Savior. Even if we stumble and fall into them, we need only to repent and He will forgive our sins and cleanse us from all unrighteousness (1 John 1:9). But don't deceive yourself—if stumbling and sinning doesn't tear your heart out and cause you to fall on your face to repent, then something is wrong.

Be very careful that your identity is not in the sin. God didn't create you "this way." A twisted, sinful nature did.

Are you someone who committed a cowardly act and repented, or is it who you are? If that is who you are, don't panic—believe in Jesus and repent of your sins (Acts 2:38). God is incredibly patient, waiting for your repentance because He wants no one to perish (2 Peter 3:9). If you are unsure of how to be saved from your sins, read John chapter 3 and believe with the level of faith that brings repentance.

Many of us assume that at death everyone will suddenly see the truth as it is. The righteous will stand, waiting for the rewards they know are coming, the carnal will be repentant for their wasted lives, and the unbelievers will beg God for mercy and another chance. That's not the picture we get from the Bible.

In stories and parables of life after death, it doesn't appear that people change after they die, at least not before judgment. In Luke 16:19–31, the rich man in torment didn't show remorse in death; he demonstrated the same arrogance that marked his life. He didn't apologize to Lazarus for ignoring his earthly plight but instead wanted to order him to perform a couple of errands.

In the parable of the three slaves (Matthew 25), the lazy slave showed no remorse. Instead he blamed the master for his wasted life and gifts. In the parable of the sheep and the goats (Matthew 25), the arrogant goats were clueless about never helping the needy on earth. Even as they were being condemned, their attitude was "What are You talking about? We're really great people!" Likewise, the humble sheep didn't realize what a big deal it was that they'd helped so many; it was simply who they were. They seemed surprised at their Master's high opinion of them. The intruder at the wedding feast (Matthew 22) was "speechless" about why he was at the party without the right wedding clothes. The man had no good works to show for himself but seemed totally unaware of his inadequacy.

Jesus gave these stories to illustrate the afterlife and instruct us on being prepared. They are mostly parables, so we don't make definitive theological conclusions from them, but in His examples, all show unchanged hearts after death. We don't see people with their eyes now opened, begging for mercy. We see arrogance, defensiveness, or humility that appear to correlate with the person's character while on earth. In essence, people seem to be the same in death as they were in life.

Father works tirelessly in this life to grow us and change us more into the likeness of His perfect Son. We assume it is only to make us better in this life, but this school of life reaches beyond just this temporal time and is molding a foundation into who we will be for eternity. We want to be like the man who sold everything he had to buy the perfect pearl (Matthew 13:45–46). Giving all now results in great blessing for all eternity.

THE REST OF THE STORY

Telling unbelievers about Jesus is hard. Like everything else, the more you do it, the better you get. Being direct and complete in presenting the gospel is always the best policy, while being sensitive to a person's specific circumstances. But no matter the circumstance, we must always present the whole gospel, including the facts about heaven and hell. In the story that starts this chapter, the main guy to whom I was witnessing asked if he could learn more, and he and a few other guys stayed up all night listening to the gospel. We didn't get to bed until 3:00 a.m. and had to be up before sunrise. The Christian man who was critical about offending people hadn't known that, nor did I tell him.

Regarding his criticism, this was a moment to listen to his concerns, carefully consider his point, and respond to him with Scripture, not justify myself. One of Satan's favorite tools is to send someone to criticize us when we're obeying God and insist we justify our actions. Never defend yourself for obeying God's Word. Respond from Scripture only. To have included the fact that several of the men stayed up all night to hear more of the gospel would've only justified that particular situation and smacked of pride. It's the kind of thing that starts arguments and pulls the saint away from godliness and toward where our enemy wants us—self-justification.

I got a job loading trucks when I was young and had to join the Teamsters union. During my few months working there, several of the long-term employees criticized me to the point of hostility because I worked too hard. The foreman finally told me that those guys had to be there day after day and year after year. I was just a college kid who would soon be off to better things. My loading too many trucks too fast exposed to the supervisors how much more they could all be doing.

Some Christians will become upset if they see you doing too much obeying of God's Word. They believe it exposes them for their own mediocrity. Always listen to critics with humility, considering that they might be correct and maybe you've missed a step somewhere, but know that if you obey God's Word with a pure heart, you can be confident. The critics insist you make them happy, but they are never our audience. We keep our eyes on Christ and Him only.

We've seen up to this point that there are two negatives: those who reject Christ are already condemned unless they repent (John 3:18), and those who place their faith in Christ and want to grow in Him will face hardship and hatred. These don't sound like good choices. But our Lord has some wonderful words for us. This is where we finally get to the amazing promises Father has made to those who live out a daring faith in this cowardly world of ours.

10

A BETTER RESURRECTION

Fight the good fight of the faith. Take hold of the eternal life to which you were called when you made your good confession in the presence of many witnesses.

1 TIMOTHY 6:12 NIV

We must remember that eternal life in the Bible is not a static entity; it is more than the initial gift of regeneration. It is a dynamic relationship with Christ Himself which grows and increases in richness as we take up our cross daily, deny ourselves, and follow Him.

DR. JOSEPH (JODY) DILLOW[1]

BEING A POLICE OFFICER IN ONE OF THE MOST VIOLENT, high-crime areas of the country brought many dangerous situations. Nearly every day, we were in vehicle or foot pursuits of dangerous criminals. Often, we'd chase a murder or deadly assault suspect into a gang-infested neighborhood. If we saw a suspect flee into one of those neighborhoods, we'd quickly set up a "perimeter." A police car would be positioned at each of the four corners and then we'd call an air unit (police helicopter) to locate where the suspect was hiding and direct the officers to his location.

Each air unit had two officers, a pilot and an observer—someone trained to locate hiding and camouflaged people. The observation officer would direct officers toward the suspect or locations where the suspect might be hiding. "Officers, turn right, climb over the fence, then walk forward 50'," was a common command. He could see what we couldn't—which yards had vicious dogs to avoid (something very common in that area of Los Angeles), where there were escape routes, or obstacles we couldn't pass.

Despite our trust in the air unit, we often failed to follow his directions. From our perspective, he often appeared to be wrong. "Turn right?" I'd sometimes think, "there's a big pile of debris over there; it looks easier to go left." I can still remember his voice often trying to correct me, urging me to listen.

Everything changed when I was invited to spend a day in an air unit. I was training a young rookie and brought him along. The LAPD had seventeen air units back then, yet there still weren't enough. We sped from one crime scene to another all night long. It was amazing to get the perspective from above. Everything was so much clearer. One could see the entire picture of all the officers, the K9 units, the perimeter; I could even easily see the suspect hiding in many cases. As the observation officer shouted down directions to the officers, I'd become frustrated watching them fail to listen. It was so clear from where we were. We could see everything; they could only see the little part they played. He was moving many pieces in unison toward victory (catching the bad guy), but if any of those pieces didn't obey exactly what he said, it made the situation much harder. When someone trusted their own instincts over the one who could see the situation much more clearly, failure loomed. If they'd just listen to him, everything would be so much easier.

I became much more effective at my job that day. I learned not to trust in my own narrow judgment but to trust the air unit's direction. In doing so, I was rewarded with victory much more often. In victory came commendations, rewards, and praise.

When we trust the God who sees all, throwing aside our flawed judgment whenever it is not aligned with Scripture, we see victory. God will reward His people, and what He rewards isn't according to the standards we use. He doesn't reward fame, success, titles, crowds, or books sales. God rewards the humble heart that diligently works to build His kingdom.

There is nothing concealed that will not be disclosed, or hidden that will not be made known. What you have said in the dark will be heard in the daylight, and what you have whispered in the ear in the inner rooms will be proclaimed from the roofs. (Luke 12:2–3 NIV)

When Jesus hands out praise, it won't be just words, though His praise would be more than any of us deserve. There will be very real consequences. Crowns, co-rulership, coheirship, intimate nicknames, and many other things we're going to look at will be awarded to the saints who have obeyed and persevered. He's also going to hand out eternal life. Didn't we all get that when we placed our faith in Him? Let's take a look.

CAN WE EARN ETERNAL LIFE?

One of the most misunderstood concepts in the Bible is that of eternal life. A primary reason for this is because so few saints understand the Old Testament. We cannot know God unless we understand and know the whole Bible, including the Old Testament. The Bible in its entirety lets us know who God is in His entirety. A wrong paradigm has led us to misinterpret Scripture time and time again, disregarding clear truths in the Bible.

If we ask most Christians whether God changed from the Old Testament to the New, I suspect almost all would say "No!" while really thinking that He has. We see the King before

Christ as angry and primarily concerned with justice. "Kill 'em all, and I'll sort 'em out later" is how we tend to perceive Him. Yet in the New Testament, we see hippie Jesus, who loves all and forgives all. We must always remember that the God of the Old Testament is Jesus.

God has been judging all people for all time. His death and resurrection paved the way for Him to judge with something other than condemnation. For those who place their faith in Him, He can now judge their works because their sin has been wiped away. To them He promises eternal life. If your idea of eternal life is that you will live forever in the presence of Jesus, you're half right.

According to Dr. Jody Dillow, the phrase *eternal life* is used forty-one times in the New Testament.[2] Whenever eternal life is mentioned in the present, it is always a gift of God's grace and always refers to living forever after we face temporal death or are raptured (John 3:16). But whenever eternal life is mentioned as something in the future, it is always conditional on works.[3] Eternal life as a promise in the present is the result of salvation. Eternal life in the future is something to be "taken hold of," as our verse to start this chapter states. It is a choice, it is action, and it is something to be earned. Obviously we're talking about two different things.

Consider Galatians 6:8: "Because the one who sows to his flesh will reap corruption from the flesh, but the one who sows to the Spirit will reap eternal life from the Spirit." This verse says that we must sow to the Spirit to reap eternal life. Does the eternal life of salvation require works such as sowing to the

Spirit? No. Do we reap (earn) eternal life? No. Therefore, Paul is talking about something else. Something earned, something gained by works.

Jesus says that if we leave behind the things we love for Him, we'll be generously rewarded and receive eternal life. "And everyone who has left houses, brothers or sisters, father or mother, children, or fields because of My name will receive 100 times more and will inherit eternal life" (Matthew 19:29). If He was speaking about salvation, His promise of eternal life is disingenuous, because it's free. He's talking about something else.

Another verse from Jesus: "The one who loves his life will lose it, and the one who hates his life in this world will keep it for eternal life" (John 12:25).

Most compellingly: "He will repay each one according to his works: eternal life to those who by persistence in doing good seek glory, honor, and immortality; but wrath and indignation to those who are self-seeking and disobey the truth" (Romans 2:6–8).

This last verse from Romans is clear that Paul is not talking about salvation. We don't need works for salvation, nor do unbelievers only get wrath and indignation. As we saw in the last chapter, their place is in the lake of fire. Indignation and wrath are for believers who have wasted their lives. Indignation is the disappointment of a Father whose child has not lived up to expectations. Wrath is from the King judging a soldier who lets others fight his battles, a worker who lets others cover his duties, an athlete who did not compete to win (all biblical analogies for believers).

We're told that the person who places their faith in Christ has unconditional acceptance by the Father. This is true; we have unconditional acceptance, but we don't have unconditional approval. When I asked my sons to help with yardwork one day, one came out to help and one didn't. When we were done, I took the son who helped to dinner and the other stayed home. Were they both my sons and did they both retain unconditional acceptance as my sons? Yes. But only one had approval at that moment and he was rewarded.

THE BETTER RESURRECTION

It takes faith alone to receive eternal life but obedience to inherit it. What does this mean? If receiving eternal life is grace but inheriting is earned, then what do we earn? Hebrews 11:35 starts us on the right path. After the Holy Spirit has pointed us to the Hall of Faith throughout chapter 11, making it clear that the followers He's looking for are people of action and faith, not politeness and rule keeping, He says: "Women received back their dead by resurrection; and others were tortured, not accepting their release, so that they might obtain a better resurrection" (NASB).

There's a better resurrection? He's not talking about the difference between salvation and condemnation, because the Holy Spirit is pointing to people willingly enduring torture and refusing release as a condition of attaining it. Therefore, He is not talking about resurrection to heaven, because lots of people will be in heaven who don't meet these criteria. Many do all they can to avoid any discomfort at all. If you've known many Christians, you realize there are many—almost all—who are certainly not in this camp. They haven't sacrificed, they haven't died to self daily, yet they are believers and will be in heaven. So the people of Hebrews 11 are willingly accepting pain and refusing release for something "better." What's better than getting to heaven?

Paul, after discussing that he had given everything to know Christ, wrote, "My goal is to know Him [Christ] and the power of His resurrection and the fellowship of His sufferings, being conformed to His death" (Philippians 3:10). Paul said he'd given up everything to gain Christ but then said his righteousness wasn't his own. He was saying that unconditional acceptance was not from his effort, but approval required he give up everything.

Paul concluded, "Assuming that I will somehow reach the resurrection from among the dead" (Philippians 3:11). Was Paul afraid he wouldn't be resurrected? Was he unsure of his salvation? Obviously not. He had just spent several verses stating what he had done to meet the requirements Christ put forward to inherit eternal life, not to receive salvation—he already had that. Paul stated to the church that he wanted the better resurrection of Hebrews 11.

As Paul discussed this resurrection, he clarified in verse 14, "I pursue as my goal the prize promised by God's heavenly call in Christ Jesus." We don't pursue salvation, and it is a gift, not a prize. The word for prize here is the victor's prize in an athletic contest.[4] Paul continued his constant references to athletics, battle, and working, with his emphasis on winning, pleasing the recruiter, and reaching the goal. As always, his point was to strain forward to be rewarded—to win the prize (1 Corinthians 9:24).

Paul wrote in 1 Corinthians 15:41–42, "There is a splendor of the sun, another of the moon, and another of the stars; for one star differs from another star in splendor. So it is with the resurrection of the dead." Resurrection from the dead will differ in splendor for each believer. A "better resurrection" is one of great splendor. It is one where we know we're heading to the judgment seat of Christ as victors—as those who have fought the good fight, run the race to win, who have accomplished the good works that were prepared ahead of time that we should walk in them. All our works will be judged at the great bema seat.

THE BEMA SEAT

The judgment seat of Christ is also called the bema seat. In ancient Greece, the culture to which Paul so often referred, the victor stood on a platform in front of the judge, where the prize was given. The prize was something visible, usually a crown or wreath, and often contained special privileges and honors, such as lifetime forgiveness of taxes, a seat on the city council, or a special gate cut into the city wall that only the victor or his family could use.

The Bible talks of specific crowns that will be awarded to believers for specific deeds and victories, consistent with the Greek ideas of honor and rewards for victors. There are five crowns specifically mentioned in the Bible, and each signifies a different level and type of victory for the Christian. These crowns will be permanent signs of victory that will mark us for eternity with special glory and all the privileges of that crown.

Crown of Life

"A man who endures trials is blessed, because when he passes the test he will receive the crown of life" (James 1:12). "Be faithful unto death, and I will give you the crown of life" (Revelation 2:10).

This crown is specifically for martyrs and those who pass the test of enduring trials. James's words here correlate to the words of Jesus. Jesus tells us to rejoice over the rewards we're earning when we endure suffering for His name: "You are blessed when they insult and persecute you and falsely say every kind of evil against you because of Me. Be glad and rejoice, because your reward is great in heaven" (Matthew 5:11–12).

This crown comes from staying faithful despite pain and suffering. It is granted to those who have been mocked, lost their friends and families, suffered loss of their status or possessions, and have even been tortured and killed, refusing to relent. Their lives, bodies, and reputations carry the scars of standing firm for the name of Jesus. The crown of life merits faithful service on the field of battle, signifying a saint who would not quit.

Crown of Righteousness

"I have fought the good fight, I have finished the race, I have kept the faith. There is reserved for me in the future the crown of righteousness, which the Lord, the righteous Judge, will give me on that day, and not only to me, but to all those who have loved His appearing" (2 Timothy 4:7–8).

Of course, all who have placed their faith in Christ have His righteousness. This is a crown for living out that righteousness on earth. It is for those who anxiously await His return and they live like it. They've given all, they've lived according to the Sermon on the Mount. More specifically, they've endured to the end. They have run through the finish line, giving all for the kingdom of God all the way through their death, whether old age, sickness, or martyrdom. There have been many examples of believers who accomplished great things in God's name over the course of their lives but succumbed to the world and didn't end well. This is given to the saint whose life and service have a singular focus of working hard until Jesus returns.

Crown of Glory

"Shepherd God's flock among you, not overseeing out of compulsion but freely, according to God's will; not for the money but eagerly; not lording it over those entrusted to you, but being examples to the flock. And when the chief Shepherd appears, you will receive the unfading crown of glory" (1 Peter 5:2–4).

This crown is for those who have been dedicated to caring for and discipling others. It is the crown of leadership—elders, pastors, ministry leaders, and so on. They are accountable to

God for how they've led and what they've taught and will be judged more strictly (James 3:1). God told Ezekiel that if he knew what to say and didn't, he would be held accountable for the sins of the people who didn't have that information (Ezekiel 3). Many Christian leaders will be held accountable if they refuse to stand against the evil in our day. Yet they will receive a great crown if they boldly stand for God's Word and teach others to do the same, despite the cost to them.

The crown of glory is hard-earned and can result in great reward but is earned by leaders who risk stricter judgment. Anyone seeking leadership in the church should do so prayerfully and humbly. It is a great responsibility and requires saints of sober courage.

Crown of Rejoicing

"For who is our hope or joy or crown of boasting in the presence of our Lord Jesus at His coming? Is it not you? For you are our glory and joy!" (1 Thessalonians 2:19–20).

This represents the people we have influenced for Christ during our life. Those we've led to salvation, discipled, and influenced will be our "glory and joy" in "the presence of our Lord Jesus." Jesus says that we can use our money to make friends for ourselves, implying that these are friends in heaven (Luke 16:9). Our better resurrection will be the people we have blessed in Christ, gathered around the bema seat, a living reward for an effective testimony on earth. Many of those getting this crown will be shocked at the number of people there to honor them, many of whom they had no idea they affected.

Billy Graham, Dwight Moody, and Charles Spurgeon will have a sea of people cheering them on; many people we never heard of will have the same. May you and I also have a great number of witnesses because of a life lived in Christ—because we accomplished the good works Father has for us to do.

Crown of Mastery

"Don't you know that the runners in a stadium all race, but only one receives the prize? Run in such a way to win the prize. Now everyone who competes exercises self-control in everything. However, they do it to receive a crown that will fade away, but we a crown that will never fade away. Therefore I do not run like one who runs aimlessly or box like one beating the air. Instead, I discipline my body and bring it under strict control, so that after preaching to others, I myself will not be disqualified" (1 Corinthians 9:24–27).

This is given to those who "run in such a way to win the prize," specifically by exercising self-control and discipline. A friend of mine who had been promiscuous before he came to know Christ in his midtwenties stayed celibate for twenty-five years until God brought him a wife. He exercised self-control because of his love of Christ; his reward was a very happy marriage now and rewards in heaven. Many believers have endured awful marriages, have daily risen early to pray, have fasted regularly, doing all to be as close to God as possible. They have disciplined their bodies (v. 27) to win the prize. Mastery here is mastery over the body and the temptations of the world, like an athlete, who is competing with complete focus and intensity, not willing to allow any pleasure or lack of discipline to dissuade him from winning. I read an article that examined why Tom Brady has played in and won so many more Super Bowls than anyone else in the NFL. The conclusion—self-discipline. The one with the most self-discipline has won the most Super Bowls. So it is in our walk with Christ.

DON'T LET YOUR CROWN BE STOLEN

"I am coming quickly. Hold on to what you have, so that no one takes your crown" (Revelation 3:11).

How is our crown taken? By not enduring to the end. Who can take our crown? Anyone who dissuades us from our relentless dedication to God and pursuit of doing His will. This is why Jesus warns us that we must love Him more than any other person on this earth. Each of the crowns has as its core the requirement that we finish well. These are victor's crowns. One doesn't get a victor's crown for competing well for most of the race and then quitting. Even the great apostle Paul worked hard to ensure he didn't lose his crown. "I discipline my body and bring it under strict control, so that after preaching to others, I myself will not be disqualified" (1 Corinthians 9:27).

THE REST OF THE STORY

The Bible is filled with stories of His choosing and rewarding the lesser person—the younger brother (Jacob), the "runt" (David), the ineloquent (Moses), the gentile (Ruth), the prostitute (Rahab, who was in the lineage of Jesus). God doesn't choose the most talented, He chooses the most obedient. He sees the big picture and He rewards those who listen to Him, even when their experience, friends, or culture say something different.

In the Gospels, we're told the story of the rich young ruler (Luke 18:18–30; Matthew 19:16–39) who came to Jesus and asked what he must do to inherit eternal life. Jesus told him to obey the commandments, to which the man replied that he had for his whole life. "You still lack one thing," Jesus said. "Sell all that you have and distribute to the poor, and you will have treasure in heaven; and come, follow Me" (Luke 18:22 NKJV).

There is an old saying that hard times make strong men, strong men make good times, good times make weak men, weak men make hard times. This saying has shown itself true in the cycles of generations and nations. It is almost a given to see a person who has struggled and worked hard to build a personal empire end up with lesser children, who don't know the pain and struggle their parents experienced to build what they take for granted. They therefore don't have the inner steel of their parents. They then raise children who are spoiled and simply see the possessions, status, and money built by their grandparents as their right. They fall apart at the slightest discomfort or pain. The steel is gone from the family. Rarely does a legacy of strength and work exist for more than a few generations.

Jesus' answer to the man sounds harsh, but He is looking for children who won't fall apart. He's looking for first-generation trailblazers, not third-generation comfort seekers.

To truly grasp what Jesus is saying, let's look at the context. This story happens immediately after Jesus corrected the disciples about the children coming to Him. They were trying to keep the children away, but Jesus told the disciples to let them come, and then He said, "Whoever does not welcome the kingdom of God like a little child will never enter it" (Luke 18:15–17). Matthew's version says that "Just then" the rich young ruler approaches.

This ruler was a follower of God. Unlike Nicodemus (John 3), who approached Jesus in the dark, this young man came to Him in front of the crowd, in the daylight. He lowered himself to talk to this group of lower-class disciples and their teacher, risking his social status. He gave every appearance of a true believer. Therefore, Jesus' answer to him differed from the one to Nicodemus, the Pharisee who snuck in from the dark to avoid scorn. Jesus instructed Nicodemus on salvation, but He instructed this man on the question asked: How to inherit eternal life? When this man said that he had kept the commandments his entire life, Jesus not only didn't correct him, but He also seemed to agree with him by saying, "You lack one thing." The one thing he lacked wasn't salvation. There was only one thing holding him back from "treasure in heaven"—money.

Love of money is really a love of what money can do and reveals the heart. For one person to receive a million dollars, he'd run out and buy a Ferrari and revel in the envious looks from people. His sin is pride, and money simply reveals it. Another might put it in the bank and take security in knowing it was there. They'd use it to no longer count on Father for their subsistence but on their savings account. Another would buy status so they could have power, and so on.

There is nothing wrong with Ferraris, savings accounts, or status, except for what they show us about our hearts, where they get in the way of total dependance on God. The next words from our Lord were to invite the man to follow Him and have treasure in heaven. Jesus knew what following Him meant. It meant imprisonment, persecution, and torture. He knew that every one of his disciples, except John, was going to experience a horrific death. If this man held on to his love of money, he wasn't prepared for what lay ahead.

When it comes to those who will not only receive eternal life but also inherit it, Jesus has no tolerance for compromise. Either we will give all or we won't. This man was on his way to heaven; we know this because Jesus never told him how to be saved. Jesus said he only lacked one thing, and that thing wasn't belief—the only thing required for salvation. Instead Jesus gave a one-sentence summary of the Sermon on the Mount: get rid of anything that is in the way of your relationship with Me.

This brings us back to the beginning of the story, the context. Jesus had just gotten done saying that we must be as little children to welcome the kingdom. A child is totally dependent on his parents. His food, comfort, freedom, and happiness are all contained in his parents. In fact, a young child isn't even aware of it; he just yields to his parents. The child isn't thinking of all the things that weigh us down as we get older.

Jesus was telling this young man that if he wanted to be able to go to the higher level—not just be "saved" but to become holy, have a life filled with the joy of the full presence of God in his heart, inherit eternal life, and earn crowns—he must get rid of all that inhibits him from being totally yielded so that he won't falter when the days of testing come, and they are coming. They were only a few years from Peter and John being thrown into prison. They were only about ten years from Jesus' brother James being martyred, at the beginning of a murderous persecution coming on the church. They were only thirty-seven years from the Roman commander Titus destroying Jerusalem and murdering a million Jews. Pain and mourning were going to come onto all of Jesus' followers shortly, but after that, joy and rewards. Jesus was telling this young man how to be a victor because that was what the man was asking. The way was too hard for that man and he left sad.

The great news is that we have a choice. We can be like the young ruler, who had status and comfort and was a believer who was unwilling to give all. Or we can be like the disciples, who placed their relationship with Jesus above all, and because they did so, He gave them the utmost status and comfort for all of eternity.

We've spent a lot of time talking about how to be holy and how to be a victor. In the next chapter, let's look at what comes from being victorious and why it is so important to encourage one another daily to stay on the path, because the suffering of this life is temporary, but the reward is great.

11

RULING WITH CHRIST AS A VICTOR

The one who is victorious and keeps My works to the
end: I will give him authority over the nations.

REVELATION 2:26

I have nothing to offer but blood, toil, tears, and
sweat. We have before us an ordeal of the most
grievous kind. You ask, what is our policy? I will
say: it is to wage war, by sea, land, and air, with all
our might and with all the strength that God can
give us; to wage war against a monstrous tyranny,
never surpassed by the dark, lamentable catalogue
of human crime. That is our policy. You ask, what
is our aim? I can answer in one word: it is victory,
victory at all costs, victory in spite of all terror,
victory, however long and hard the road may be.

WINSTON CHURCHILL[1]

NEVILLE CHAMBERLAIN WAS A NICE GUY. HE WAS SO NICE that as the prime minister of Great Britain he gave the leader of Germany, Adolf Hitler, control over the German-speaking countries of Europe without a shot fired. Hitler was a problem. When he took over Germany in 1933, it had worthless currency, rampant unemployment, a terrible economy, and no military. By the time Chamberlain signed the Munich Agreement in 1938, Hitler was striking fear in the hearts of leaders across the globe. In only five and a half years, Germany went from toiling in abject poverty to standing on the doorstep of ruling Europe.

The British cheered Chamberlain. Hitler was increasingly aggressive, and Chamberlain had given them the appearance of peace. Giving evil tyrants free stuff to beg for peace has never worked, but England hoped this time was different. Hitler, now controlling a larger swath of Europe without having to go to war, was able to concentrate on building the Nazi-led military without any distractions until, one year later, they invaded Poland and started World War II.

In May 1940, eight months into the war, the British elected Winston Churchill as prime minister. Unlike Neville Chamberlain, Churchill was not a nice guy. He was unpopular, given to great bouts of depression, and unwaveringly dedicated to victory, no matter the costs. The British were still wavering—victory at what cost? Couldn't something else be done to appease Hitler? The monstrosity of Hitler was still unknown. He was a tyrant, a warmonger, a man who was discriminating against gypsies and Jews, but knowledge of Auschwitz was a long way away. Churchill saw what his countrymen couldn't. He saw what was to come—Hitler's maniacal drive for power that would lead to the horrors of the Holocaust and tens of millions of people killed in war.

In the same month Churchill took over as prime minister, British troops in France retreated to Dunkirk and were in danger of being slaughtered on the beaches by the Germans. Churchill's cabinet insisted he go to Hitler for peace. He refused. Over three hundred thousand soldiers were evacuated from the beaches in a move many considered a miracle. Before they could celebrate, Germany took France. Despite having a much larger and well-funded military, the French soldiers were overrun. The German army marched from Belgium to Paris in only weeks. The British were counting on the French. The ease with which the Germans marched through them was shocking. Many in Churchill's cabinet and Parliament again insisted he go to Hitler for peace. Still he refused.

With the Nazis now controlling France, they bombed London relentlessly. Churchill understood that his main duty was to daily remind the British of the evil they faced and the need to fight on. It was no easy task as, night after night, German planes dropped bombs on the homes of the innocent, the nameless and faceless. Explosions took lives and livelihoods, destroying homes and businesses and dreams.

It was clear Britain couldn't stand forever. They needed the United States to get into the war, but there was no guarantee of that. The people of the US were in no mood for another European war and weren't sure if there was a good side. One of the greatest heroes in America, Charles Lindbergh, was pushing for the US to side with Germany. Most of the 1930s had seen Father Coughlin, a popular radio personality, spew anti-Jewish hatred across America. That had worked, and there was a strong streak of anti-Semitism running through the US that made many sympathetic to Hitler's discrimination against the Jews.

Churchill relentlessly led, encouraged, and refused to waver as his beloved country was destroyed around him and many of those in power pushed him to make peace with Hitler. Then Churchill was offered the perfect way out. In June 1940, Churchill was offered everything a leader who wasn't relentlessly driven for victory could have asked for. Hitler asked for peace.

The bombings would stop; no more Englishmen would die. Churchill could declare victory. Germany would control Europe under Hitler's growing murderous tyranny, but Britain and its empire would be left alone. Hitler had made it clear that his ambitions were to the east and he didn't want to destroy Britain. Churchill was pressed from all sides to take the peace. The bombings, the death, the destruction would all stop. They'd stop for the English, that is—Churchill knew Hitler wanted peace so that he could invade the Soviet Union. With the entirety of his army concentrated to the east, he'd run over Russia. And then, with the entire united army of Europe behind him, he'd turn back on Great Britain. The peace would be temporary and then Great Britain would experience the full power and rage of a madman.

Despite the chorus of voices desperate for temporary peace and comfort, Churchill refused. Churchill persevered through the dark months of 1941 until the Japanese made their big mistake at Pearl Harbor, and the United States entered the war. Churchill never relented, he never compromised, he never gave in . . . and he saved the world.

ONWARD CHRISTIAN SOLDIERS

The Bible, especially the writings of Paul, is filled with calls for Christians to be victors (Revelation 2:26, 3:21, 21:7). Another word used is *overcomers*. To be an overcomer is to resist the pleasure of the world, the security of money, the lure of power, the fear of the unknown, the approval of family and friends, and the temptation to be lazy, using God's gifts on our own ambitions. Winning takes the passion, perseverance, and patience we've discussed.

I can think of no greater example than Winston Churchill. He stood against all odds to fight evil, tirelessly encouraging those weaker than him (which was everyone), never relenting despite the criticism. This is how the victors are to live in Christ. Many in Churchill's cabinet and in Parliament were on his side, but they begged him to make the temporary peace that would have been their destruction. They were good Englishmen, but they weren't victors.

So it is with us. There are many "good" Christians who are on our side, but their advice is to seek compromise and to take an easier path that would cost us the world. They'd cost us our crowns; they'd cost us intimacy with Christ for eternity. They are our loved ones and friends; our spouses and children; our mothers and fathers. They don't want to see us work so hard and suffer. They have good intentions, but they can't see the whole picture. Their eyes are not fixed on victory.

I had a close friend, whom I had discipled for many years, come over one night to get advice. He was in a bad situation that was not of his own making. In tears, he told me an awful story. My heart broke for him, and I had a solution for him that was not from the Lord. I desperately wanted to give him advice on a shortcut to get out of his situation, but I heard God's voice screaming in my head to keep my mouth shut. I never did give him that advice but instead watched him suffer for a few more years. Eventually he started to pull away from me.

The situation finally collapsed, and my friend came out of it with great integrity. He suffered through an awful trial, never relenting in his trust in God. When it was over, we grabbed some steaks and I told him about the bad advice I almost gave him. "I know," he said. "I could see it in your eyes. I know how much you love me and how badly you wanted to give me an easy way out, but I had to go through it to the end. That's why I pulled away for a while. I was afraid you'd give me permission to compromise."

"Yeah, man," I said. "You came to me for godly counsel, and I almost cost you the growth you found in Christ and the rewards you earned by standing so steadfast." We laughed about it but my statement was true. My compassion for him almost led me to seek his relief rather than his best.

"If we endure, we will also reign with Him" (2 Timothy 2:12). Notice the condition of the promise. We will reign with Him *if* we're faithful. Are all Christians faithful? No. Only some will reign with Him. God is looking for saints who will rule and judge with Him. See the verse that starts this chapter. We're told that we'll judge angels (1 Corinthians 6:3). The Father side of God loves all believers as His children, but the King is looking for those children who are worthy to judge His angels and to rule nations.

We're growing in Christ and proving our mettle now in order to receive not only the victor's crowns we saw in the last chapter but the ability to rule with Christ. Romans 8:17 says that we can be coheirs with Christ and share in His glory *if* we share in His sufferings in this life. Ruling with Him comes at great cost in this life but great privilege in the next.

PRIVILEGES OF THE VICTOR

Pastor Erwin Lutzer wrote in his book *Your Eternal Reward*, "Those who rule with Christ are overcomers, those who have successfully conquered the challenges of this life. . . . They have resisted the threefold seduction of pleasure, possessions, and power."[2] We see that one of the great honors of being a victor or overcomer is to receive honor through crowns based on specific victories in our lives. The victor will be a coheir with Jesus, resulting in many privileges that are the symbols that God trusts us to reign with Jesus and to judge angels.

Coheirship with Christ (Romans 8:17; Colossians 3:23–25)

It's been emphasized in this book the need to know and understand the Old Testament. Having knowledge of only the New Testament can lead to misunderstandings, because it was written to people who had only the Old Testament at the time and had a solid understanding of it. The New Testament is meant to build on the foundation of the Old, to augment it, to continue the story of Messiah. The Bible, in its entirety, shows us who God is.

One of the most often misunderstood of these issues is the many references to us being heirs or coheirs with Christ. Israel's entry into the promised land is seen as a foreshadowing of our entrance into heaven. It is repeatedly called their inheritance given by God, just as our entrance into heaven is called an inheritance.

"Now if we are children, then we are heirs—heirs of God and co-heirs with Christ, if indeed we share in his sufferings in order that we may also share in his glory" (Romans 8:17 NIV). Believers will be heirs, but only those who suffer with Him will be coheirs with Christ. According to Dillow, the translation of this verse is difficult but means something like "On one hand heirs, on the other hand coheirs." What's the difference? If I made out a will and left some money to a few friends and relatives, leaving the bulk of the estate to my kids to divide up equally, the friends and relatives are heirs but my kids are coheirs. The first group inherited a portion of what I had. My kids have inherited all of the rights and privileges of my estate. Jesus is God's Son. All Christians are heirs and have the opportunity for heaven. Those who "share in His sufferings in order that we may also share in His glory" can be coheirs with the Son.

I had a close friend in his seventies who had a long and painful bout with cancer. He had a biological son and two adopted children. Elliette and I visited him often during his many bad episodes that landed him in the hospital. We never failed to see his biological son by his side, even though the son was a missionary in Asia. But never did we see his adopted children. When I asked him about it, he said that even though they'd been adopted as babies, they'd separated themselves from him and his wife as soon as they reached adulthood. There was no relationship. They forfeited the relationship with their father to the point of even ignoring him while he suffered and died.

Jesus is the Son of God. We are adopted children. God the Father is looking for children who bear the image of His Son. They seek intimacy with Him by visiting Him in the hospital (Matthew 25:35–36), by feeding Him when He's hungry, by standing for His name, no matter the circumstance (Matthew 10:33). God the King is looking for children to reign with His Son. As a righteous King, He's only looking for those who have proven themselves worthy of such an honor. He will not entrust the rule of His kingdom or the judgment of His angels to the mediocre.

Greater Intimacy

Coheirship necessarily implies greater intimacy with Father. All the special privileges are portions of the closeness we can have with God for eternity.

Father has new names for those who are special to Him. He called Simon Peter the "rock"; the way Peter's new name was given, it was almost as if Jesus was saying, "chip off the ole block." Jesus was the chief cornerstone and Peter was the rock. Saul became Paul, Sarai became Sarah, Jacob became Israel.

How great it is that Jesus says in Revelation 2:17, "I will give the victor some of the hidden manna. I will also give him a white stone, and on the stone a new name is inscribed that no one knows except the one who receives it." Jesus will have a special name that only He calls us and only He knows. What an honor to have that level of closeness with Him, our coheir. Will everyone get such friendship with Jesus? No. According to Revelation 2:17, just the victors.

In Revelation 3:12, Jesus says, "The victor: I will make him a pillar in the sanctuary of My God, and he will never go out again. I will write on him the name of My God." Revelation shows that there will be nations and the new Jerusalem, from where Christ will reign. People will come and trade and live in different portions of the city and have different levels of access to Father. Being a pillar that will never leave signifies having a level of closeness with God that we will never be out of touch with Him, and we will have the honor of wearing His name.

Judging Nations and Angels

"Then I saw thrones, and people seated on them who were given authority to judge" (Revelation 20:4).

> They probed into what person or time the Spirit of Christ within them was indicating when he testified beforehand about the sufferings appointed for Christ and his subsequent glory. They were shown that they were serving not themselves but you, in regard to the things now announced to you through those who proclaimed the gospel to you by the Holy Spirit sent from heaven—things angels long to catch a glimpse of. (1 Peter 1:11–12 NET)

According to 1 Peter, the angels watch over us with great consideration. They are fascinated by the unique ability of humans to exercise faith moment to moment. We're frail, trapped in a weak, decaying body that has strange yearnings and makes us do weird things to satisfy them. Yet those who overcome will someday judge the angels (1 Corinthians 6:3). The angels look on us with intrigue. What is it that we have that would fascinate the angels?

Faith. The courage to believe in things unseen, to put our deepest trust in something we cannot fully understand, is a profound mystery of being human. It is unique in all creation, whether among principalities throughout the universe or creatures here on earth. The frail body-trapped humans will someday have a special intimacy and position with the Creator because they overcame their weakness through faith. Those overcomers will be the judges of angels. All the humans? No. Just the ones who overcame. Those who were trapped in pleasing that flesh and acquiescing to the world remained in their frailty and will reap from their choice. They will be in heaven but will be the "least."

Eternal Honor (Matthew 5:19–20)

As we saw in the chapter on the Sermon on the Mount, Jesus says some will be the least in the kingdom of heaven and some the greatest. Jesus said, "And whoever gives just a cup of cold water to one of these little ones because he is a disciple—I assure you: He will never lose his reward!" (Matthew 10:42).

In that passage, Jesus had just finished saying that we can receive a prophet's reward and a righteous man's reward, and He now pointed to a reward for even the slightest act of service done. But He gave two requirements: we must first be disciples, and we must have done it because we're disciples, not out of pride, by manipulation, or for the praise of others. Our hearts must have done it from pure love of the Father with the sole intention of serving others.

God will not forget a single thing we've done out of love for Him. The following verse really nails this home:

At that time those who feared the LORD spoke to one another. The LORD took notice and listened. So a book of remembrance was written before Him for those who feared Yahweh and had high regard for His name. "They will be Mine," says the LORD of Hosts, "a special possession on the day I am preparing. I will have compassion on them as a man has compassion on his son who serves him." (Malachi 3:16–17)

We see special honor reserved for the victors: coheirship, crowns, wearing God's name, a special place in the temple, rulership, getting a special nickname from Jesus, judging angels. Are you a victor? Do you love Him? Have you offered all to be close to Him? Is there anything you hold back? Possessions, money, spouse, kids, even your reputation? Would you give all to know Him more? These are the requirements of discipleship—the road to becoming a victor—not of salvation. God says, "Be holy, because I am holy" (1 Peter 1:16). The road is wide for those who would believe but do not "share in His sufferings"; it is narrow indeed for those who want the closest of intimacy with Him, but the benefits are eternal. All who believe will be in heaven but not all will have the same place. Some will be the "greatest" and some the "least."

The best news of all is that it's never too late to start. Moses was eighty before he figured it out. We're seeing that it is of great value to have a daring faith in this cowardly world.

THE REST OF THE STORY

On July 5, 1945, less than two months after the surrender of Nazi Germany, Churchill lost reelection in a landslide. The man who had stood against the political powers of Great

Britain, resisted the cries of his people, and stared down Adolf Hitler, rescuing the world from a monster, was thrown out of office by the very people he'd saved.

History has been kind to Churchill, but in his time he was devastated by the lack of gratitude from the world.[3] Churchill was the greatest leader of the twentieth century, yet the world used him and then rejected him when his usefulness was over. The new prime minister, Clement Attlee, proclaimed that Churchill was unqualified to be a peacetime leader. He was a peacemaker, and Britain was looking for a peacekeeper. *Thanks for saving the world, now get lost* was the message Churchill heard.

For those who have given all, recognition will likely not come in this world, and if it does, it will not be adequate. When true recognition does come, it will be in front of all the rulers of the universe and every believer we knew on earth. It will come from the great King, our Father and Creator, and will be accompanied by rewards, rulership, and crowns. Let's keep our eyes on Him. There is nothing in this world that is worth even the slightest compromise that would cost us closeness with our Father.

LET'S GET MARRIED!

*Then I heard something like the voice of a vast multitude,
like the sound of cascading waters, and like the rumbling
of loud thunder, saying: Hallelujah, because our Lord
God, the Almighty, has begun to reign! Let us be glad,
rejoice, and give Him glory, because the marriage of the
Lamb has come, and His wife has prepared herself. She
was given fine linen to wear, bright and pure. For the
fine linen represents the righteous acts of the saints.*

REVELATION 19:6–8

*I believe that one reason why the church
of God at this present moment has so little
influence over the world is because the world
has so much influence over the church.*

CHARLES SPURGEON[1]

MY WIFE, ELLIETTE, AND A FRIEND OF HERS WENT TO A large prayer gathering at our state capitol a few years ago. I called her that afternoon to see how it went and she informed me that they went for the beginning but didn't stay. There were tens of thousands of people there, it was an incredible showing, but there wasn't room for everyone as the crowd spilled out across the streets.

There was a large homeless camp near the capitol, so in order to make room for two more people at the prayer gathering, Elliette and her friend walked over to McDonald's, bought one hundred hamburgers, and started sharing the gospel and feeding people. They had mentally disturbed people screaming in their faces, filthy people looking for hugs, and one demon-possessed man telling them he was going to kill them. Neither woman was dissuaded; they were used to it. Amid the commotion, gratitude, screaming, and threats, they led four people to Christ. They spent several hours discipling them and telling them where they could find a church that would help.

I listened with my usual gratitude to be married to such a woman of God and concern over all the risks of exercising such love. Elliette wasn't reporting something she was proud of; it was simply her day. She's had many days just like that one. She doesn't do it to feel good about herself or be seen by anyone (in fact, no one ever knew of this until I put it into this book);

she does it because her love for Christ spills over into a need to express it to anyone who will let her. We'll see in this chapter that, though Elliette does none of this to gain anything, even from God, it will affect her eternity.

THE BRIDE HAS MADE HERSELF READY

The great culmination of the church age is the wedding feast of the Son of God. Jesus has His bride, which will come out of His church. His marriage feast marks the beginning of His rule on earth during the millennial kingdom as He and His bride will rule from Jerusalem. As the Bible draws to a close, Jesus, now wed, shouts an invitation together with His bride. Jointly they invite all who are thirsty to drink the living water (Revelation 22:17).

It is important to note that this is not the end of the world. It is the end of the church age and the beginning of the millennial age. Armageddon is often referred to as the end of the world, but this is not the case. The only thing Armageddon ends is the current age in which we live. God has dealt with people in distinctively different ways throughout history. The time before the flood, from the flood to Abraham, from Abraham to Moses, and so on. This shows us that God has had very different ways of dealing with people at different times of history.

This is important because we live in the second-to-last age, the age of the church. This is the time of betrothal for Jesus to

His bride. In Israel, after a man and woman were engaged, the man would return to his father's house and build a room onto it for his bride. When it was finished and the house was ready for her, he would return. She had no way of knowing how long he'd be gone or how long the work was taking. When he did return, it was with a great shout, trumpets blaring. Then the wedding feast would start. The groom expected to find his bride anxiously awaiting his return, ready for the wedding feast.

We see so many of Jesus' words in this. He is coming at a time we don't know. He'll come with a great shout. He expects us to be ready. He has gone away to His Father's house where there are many rooms, to prepare a place for us. The wedding feast is the great celebration—the culmination of human history, the celebration of His sacrifice for His bride, and the beginning of the fulfillment of all the rest of the prophecies of Scripture. Messiah will reign on earth, Israel will be brought to the full glory that was always intended, and those who have served Him faithfully will reign with Him.

WARNINGS FOR THE WEDDING GUESTS

Jesus has some serious warnings for us if we want to be at the feast. Let's look at several parables Jesus tells us about His kingdom and being in His service. They are scary and violent, and we often deal with them by telling ourselves that He's talking about unbelievers. He isn't. He's talking about us.

Let's look at this first parable in its entirety and then

summarize several others for the sake of brevity. We'll see some themes that run through them all, to which we'd be wise to pay careful attention. In Matthew 24, Jesus gave warnings about the end times. He went back and forth with warnings about the impending destruction of Jerusalem that happened in AD 70 and the end of our current age when He will return and rule from Jerusalem.

Keep Working (Matthew 24:45–51)

As He finished, He asked a question:

> Who then is a faithful and sensible slave, whom his master has put in charge of his household, to give them food at the proper time? That slave whose master finds him working when he comes will be rewarded. I assure you: He will put him in charge of all of his possessions. But if that wicked slave says in his heart, "My master is delayed," and starts to beat his fellow slaves, and eats and drinks with drunkards, that slave's master will come on a day he does not expect and at an hour he does not know. He will cut him to pieces and assign him a place with the hypocrites. In that place there will be weeping and gnashing of teeth.

Jesus is giving a stern warning. In this story, God is the master, and His people are represented by the slave who is awaiting the master's return. This is a question of choice. Jesus is talking about one person; he either chooses to be faithful and is found working, or he has chosen to be wicked and is exploiting his fellow slaves. For the slave who is working, the story reiterates so much of what we've already discussed. He will be rewarded and will be given rule. But what of the slave who chooses self?

Jesus said we are either a slave of sin and Satan or a slave of His (we saw earlier that we can rise from slave to friend through obedience). The person in the story is a slave waiting for his master who is away for a long time. This is an illustration about a Christian and the life he lives after salvation. It can't be about a non-Christian because unbelievers aren't waiting for Jesus and don't see Him as their Master. The Christian who has decided to live for self beats his fellow slaves. This illustrates a Christian who lets others do the work assigned to him. A slave would beat his fellow slaves to get them to do what is his to do. Eating and drinking with drunkards is typically meant as seeking comfort in this life with no regard to responsibility. The wicked slave represents a carnal Christian who lives for himself and exploits his fellow believers. He isn't anxiously awaiting his master's return.

What does it mean that he's "cut . . . to pieces"? Hebrews 4:12 says that the Word of God is so sharp it separates even soul and spirit. Revelation 1 describes Jesus as having a sword coming from His mouth, and He is later seen fighting against nations with the sharp sword proceeding from His mouth (Revelation 19:15). The Christian who lives for himself and is not about the King's business will be cut to pieces by the Word of God. Where is the place with the hypocrites in the outer darkness? We'll get to that in a bit.

Stay Passionate (Matthew 25:1–13)

Immediately after this story of choice Jesus told another parable—about ten virgins. Five were sensible and five foolish. The five sensible virgins were invited into the wedding feast, but the foolish virgins were shut out. When they asked to come in, the master said he never knew them. The master again represents God. The word for "knew" is one of intimacy, communicating a deep personal relationship.

If someone accuses a close friend of mine of a terrible crime, I might say, "There's no way he did it; I know him." I mean I'm deeply familiar with his character. If someone accuses a casual acquaintance, I'd say, "Wow! I didn't really know that guy." That's the idea here. The foolish virgins had done nothing to prepare for eternity, or to build an intimate relationship with the Master. Jesus summed up the story by warning us to be on the alert because we don't know when He's returning.

The theme is the same as the story about the slave with a choice. In the first parable, a Christian who is lazy and wicked is cut to pieces and assigned a place with the hypocrites. In the second, the foolish virgins aren't said to be wicked, just unprepared. They are shut out. These represent people who were nice Christians. They kept the man-made "rules" that someone somewhere told them they were supposed to obey. Jesus doesn't want rule followers; He wants people who are passionate about knowing Him.

Jesus will judge for faithfulness and hard work, looking into our hearts for our motives. These believers didn't work hard, and in the moments when they appeared to, their motives weren't pure. They wanted to be seen; they wanted credit from people. They gave generously as long as their name was put on the building. They helped the poor and made sure everyone knew about it. They are unworthy of wearing the "fine linen, bright and pure." They've done nothing to build a genuine relationship with the Master, and when they beg to be let in to the wedding feast despite their lack of preparation, He says those awful words, "I don't know you."

Don't Waste Your Talent (Matthew 25:14–30)

Now we're in the third parable of warning. This is the well-known parable of the talents given to three slaves. One was given five talents, one three talents, and one a single talent. Each was given the money to invest according to his ability. Their master went on a long journey, and immediately the first two got to work while the third buried his money. When the master came back, he praised the first two slaves and put them in charge of many things. The third he pronounced to be an evil, lazy slave and threw him into the outer darkness, where there is weeping and gnashing of teeth. Yet again the master is God, and the slaves are Christians at the judgment seat of Christ.

There it is again—praise, rewards, and authority granted to those at work while their Master is gone, those who are anticipating and prepared for His return. For those who received His grace but spent their lives in unrepentant sin, selfishly living for self, we see outer darkness, weeping, and being shut out. They were like a bride that betrayed her fiancé while he was gone preparing a place for her. Luke 19 has a parallel story where the righteous slaves were rewarded by being put in charge of cities and the master slaughtered those who refused his rule (these would be the unbelievers since they rejected Him as their King, remaining slaves of sin and Satan).

Be Clothed in Good Works (Matthew 22:1–14)

The first part of this parable is obvious in its meaning, but the end has perplexed many people. A king threw a wedding feast for his son and invited guests to come, but they all turned him down. They gave excuses that are overtly silly, insulting the king and making it obvious they didn't value the son. Then they beat and killed the king's messengers. The king destroyed the people who would have been the guests. These guests represent unbelievers—those who have rejected the king's free invitation and then persecuted those who brought the message of the gospel.

The king then filled the banquet hall with everyone else, both good and evil. These represent Christians. They are at the wedding feast. The parable thus far is familiar. The unbelievers rejected the king and persecuted his messengers, and those deemed unworthy were invited because of the king's goodwill. Then the story takes an odd turn:

> But when the king came in to see the guests, he noticed a man there who was not wearing wedding clothes. He asked, "How did you get in here without wedding clothes, friend?"

The man was speechless. Then the king told the attend-
ants, "Tie him hand and foot, and throw him outside, into
the darkness, where there will be weeping and gnashing of
teeth." For many are invited, but few are chosen. (Matthew
22:11–14 NIV)

Here is a man at the feast who doesn't belong. The fact that
he's there shows that he is a Christian. The king is so offended
at his lack of proper clothing that he has him tied up and cast
out. The king has been completely inclusive, inviting good
and evil, yet is furious at this guest because he doesn't have on
wedding clothes. It seems like many of the guests there would
have lacked good clothes since they came from all walks of life,
including poverty.

In order to understand the king's offense, we must understand what the clothes are. In Revelation 6, we see a huge
multitude just raptured to heaven, all wearing white robes.
The robes are white, the angel explains, because they've been
dipped in the blood of the Lamb—representing the covering of
their sins. The bride wears fine linen, pure and bright, which
represents good works. This man lacks the right clothes and
seems to represent Christians who died without good works
(fine linen) and in unrepentant sin (white robes).

It aligns with the other parables of people thrown out
where there is weeping and gnashing of teeth, the wicked, lazy
slave, and the slave who beats his fellow slaves and lives this
life only for himself.

SHUT OUT

All of these point to exclusion from the wedding feast. The outer darkness refers to being outside the brightly lit feast. The weeping and gnashing of teeth show extreme remorse and anger. Those without the proper clothes, who are not prepared for the coming of the Groom, will be excluded from the greatest moment in human history. They'll see Paul and Abraham, Rahab and Mary, Moses and Peter, Billy Graham and Saint Augustine all at the great feast. All have been counted worthy. All are friends of Jesus. All are coheirs and will reign with Him. Members of the bride, ruling with Jesus from Jerusalem.

THE GREAT ENGAGEMENT

The church age has been the long betrothal of the Son and His bride. He went away to His Father to prepare a place for her. When He returns, it will be with a shout to bring the last believers home so that the bride will be complete, and the great celebration can begin.

This world is not our home. What we see doesn't satisfy. We ache for something more, something just out of reach. What we ache for is the return of Christ, when we will be brought to our true home. So often we try to satisfy this yearning through relationships, accomplishments, competition, or materialism. Try as we might, we can't satisfy the deep yearning for something we can't quite reach. We are called to lives of delayed gratification.

Waiting is hard and many people wander off the narrow path looking to satisfy that ache in this world. We want our rewards now, before they've been earned through persevering to the end. Those who wander off the path, looking for fulfillment here rather than preparing for the coming of the Groom, end up like the foolish virgins. They will be shut out from the wedding feast. Some wander so far that they become enticed and then trapped in sin, forgetting their duty, becoming like the lazy slave. They will be cast out where they will have intense remorse. The most tragic are those who no longer even remember who they are. They are consumed with sin, using and exploiting others. They will be bound hand and foot, cut into pieces, and thrown out with the hypocrites. Jesus' parables say that all three groups will be shut out. The first two groups will suffer loss, but the last group will be cut to pieces by the truth of His Word.

Jesus is passionate about a bride who waits anxiously for His return when the time of her waiting is over. The keys to discipleship are passion, perseverance, and patience. There is glory in the waiting, exercising self-control, and never relenting. It hones us and reminds us that we are not in control. Rather than do things to distract from the waiting (which always include increasing our loyalty to this world) and make ourselves feel like we're in control, we work, building up other believers so that we can encourage the bride, spreading the good news of the gospel to fulfill the entirety of the bride.

THE SECOND ADAM

"Then he said to me, 'Write: Blessed are those who are invited to the wedding feast of the Lamb'" (Revelation 19:9 NASB). The angel, having just announced the appearance of the bride, now says that those who are invited are blessed. That's strange. Why would a bride need to be invited to her own wedding—unless some of the Christians there aren't in the bride?

The church, in its entirety, is the body of Christ. Every believer makes up the body, warts and all. Some are warts, ugly representatives of the body, who take up space without benefiting the body at all. Yet they are there, they have believed, and they are forgiven. Some are hands and feet. They are at work, blessing others.

If the whole church is the body, then the whole church can't be the bride. A man doesn't marry his own body. Jesus is called the Second (or last) Adam in the Bible (1 Corinthians 15:45–49). The first Adam was our representative, choosing sin that doomed us all to a sinful nature and causing all earthly creation to come under a curse. The sinful curse came through Adam, not Eve. God told Adam not to eat from the forbidden tree, not Eve. Jesus was born of a virgin because the sinful nature passed through the seed of a man. Because Jesus was born only of woman, we got a new shot. A new representative was born without the cursed nature. We were able to choose God and not sin.

Where did the first Adam's bride come from? His whole body? No. Just a remnant. Just one rib. In the same way, the bride will be a remnant of the body. She will come out of the body, the church, but will not be the entire body, only those counted worthy, who make up the "fine linen, bright and pure, which . . . represents the righteous acts of the saints."

Thus, those that the master "knows" will participate in the culmination of the great wedding feast and those He doesn't "know" will not. What a blessing to share in the great joy of the Father! "Many are called but few are chosen." He calls to many, choosing only those who seek relationship with Him in faith, the same faith the angels marvel at.

THE REST OF THE STORY

The story about Elliette that starts this chapter is not a rare one. She has cooked meals for the homeless and delivered them on cold nights. She often takes calls in the middle of the night from sobbing women she barely knows who need prayer. She has led two different Nigerian men to Christ who tried to defraud her on eBay, and two Indian men who called with scams to get money and instead got the gospel. One sent her a picture of himself proudly holding up the Bible he bought the next day. She still disciples him over texts.

Elliette doesn't really think about these things when she does them. A man tries to steal from her on eBay and, rather than get angry, she sees a soul that needs Jesus. Thieves from another continent are one thing, but sometimes her love of serving the needy can be terrifying to her husband (that would be me).

One day she came home to tell me of two men she'd pulled her car over to help. They were wheeling a shredded tire up the highway. Pulling over to help people in need and sharing the gospel isn't anything new for Elliette. She often has stories, like of the time she stopped on the freeway for a car full of teenagers on a cross-country trip who'd been stranded for hours with no one offering to help. Close to tears, with no idea what to do, they simply sat on the freeway waiting for something to happen. Elliette happened. She called AAA and waited while their flat tire was fixed and they were on their way.

But her story of the men was different. They were two men in the country illegally whom she loaded into her minivan, along with their tire, and brought to a mechanic, where she bought them a new tire and told them about Christ. They were a captive audience, after all.

As she told me the story, my police experiences came rushing to mind in an instant and it showed on my face. "I wasn't worried about my safety for a minute, Ken," she said. "I could feel the Lord leading me to help those men."

I nodded, knowing Elliette hears the Lord's voice much more than I do. She practically has a direct line. Nevertheless, she just loaded two strange men into her car, and I'd had plenty of experience on the LAPD seeing what strange men can do to an innocent woman. "Baby," I said, "if you ever find yourself in that position again . . . Well, a man's gotta unfasten his seat belt to attack you. If he does, you hit the gas with all you've got, and when you get to about a hundred, slam on the brakes. He'll go right through the windshield."

"Ken," she said calmly, "I'm trying to lead them to Christ."

"Yes," I said, "but if they attack you, I'm telling you how to send them to Him quickly."

She didn't think I was funny.

A CUP OF WATER

He will repay each one according to his works.

ROMANS 2:6

Did you exchange a walk-on part in
the war for a lead role in a cage?

PINK FLOYD, "WISH YOU WERE HERE"

GENERAL JERRY BOYKIN IS ONE OF THE GREATEST AMERICAN heroes to ever exist. Jerry was a Green Beret, Army Ranger, and one of the first Delta Force (the finest fighting force in the world) members. While fighting in Grenada, he was shot through the torso with a .50-caliber bullet and lived after God miraculously healed him. Jerry was assigned to chase down Pablo Escobar, the notorious drug king, which he did, twice. The first time, Escobar escaped the Colombian authorities to whom Jerry had given him, so he chased him down again. Jerry took Manuel Noriega into custody and was the commanding officer at the Black Hawk Down incident in Mogadishu. His résumé sounds like an adventure novel.

Jerry and I have spent many hours fishing, praying together around campfires, and smoking cigars in the mountains. He is not only a great American hero, but he's also a great hero of the faith. I got a chance to witness how a man whose identity is completely based on his sonship in the kingdom of God rather than earthly accomplishments responds when he's wronged. Jerry had just been fired from his job at Hampden-Sydney College, where he served as a professor, having made some controversial statements against the city of Charlotte for voting to allow trans men to use women's bathrooms.

It was a national news story that got bigger when the students at the college marched in support of General Boykin and then the alumni started calling the new president insisting that he be reinstated. Jerry and I were fishing when the president of the college called him, offering him his job back. Jerry was incredibly humble, calling him sir and thanking him.

I stayed quiet about it until we were sitting around a fire that night listening to the river rush by. "Man, Jerry, you were so gracious toward that president," I said. "I can't believe you didn't spike the ball in his face at least a little."

He chuckled. "I just figure maybe he'll see Jesus in my response, Ken. I mean, what do I get out of being prideful? I'd rather he see Jesus in this whole thing than me."

I considered what I was going to say next, weighing whether it was helpful, finally deciding it was. "Jerry, my guess is that he's just waiting for the media attention and the passion of the alums to die down. When it does, he's going to fire you anyway."

Jerry stared into the fire for a while, dragging on his cigar. Then, in his thick North Carolina drawl, he said, "Yeah . . . I think you're right." Jerry's contract was not renewed at the end of that school year. He could have held a press conference. He could have turned it into a major news story again. Instead he never said a word about it.

Jerry was a man patiently waiting for acknowledgment from his Father in heaven, not wasting his efforts on the temporal satisfaction of his ego. Everything we see in creation requires passion, perseverance, and patience to get the reward. The extent to which we exercise those is the extent to which we'll be rewarded. Some give little and they get little. So it is in our walk with Christ. Everything in our existence shows the same pattern.

We live in a world of delayed gratification, and gratification comes from work. Everything points to it. The birth of a child comes from nine months of waiting followed by great pain. Getting in shape comes from months of hard work and strain. Building a business, learning to play an instrument, mastering a new language, all take passion, perseverance, and patience. Even building a happy marriage is a lifetime of sacrifice and hard work.

Salvation comes from His grace through His gift of faith. The moment of salvation is when our spiritual hearts begin to beat. It is the beginning of life. We're babies, newly born into the family, but we must grow, and as we grow, we must work. There are countless temptations, false teachers, an enemy who is trying to push us off course, and numerous people who would steal our crowns, but the crowns, wedding feast, privileges, and rulership come to the one who works and perseveres.

Jesus has given us the formula to succeed and draw close to Him in the Gospels and specifically in the Sermon on the Mount. Let us, like a runner straining for the goal, like a soldier relentlessly dedicated to victory, like a worker who won't rest until the project is finished, never cease from pursuing to please our Father in heaven. He promised that He wouldn't forget even a cup of water given to a child in His name (Matthew 10:42).

THE REST OF THE STORY

Remember the story about Jake Gordon that started chapter 2? He was asked at his retirement party in 1992 if he regretted hurting his career to get that police officer his job back. It was pointed out that the lieutenant who betrayed him had retired as a commander, near the very top of the LAPD, while Gordon had only made Captain 3, one step below. The question was if Jake felt as though he'd lost.

Captain Gordon thought about that for a minute and then shook his head. "No," he said. "He retired as a commander, but I retired as a man."

I spoke at Captain Gordon's funeral recently. It was well attended by the leadership of the LAPD. An honor guard played bagpipes and presented his daughter with a flag. The chief of police honored him with a letter. Many came to hail the great man who made such a sacrifice to stand for righteousness. His daring faith was known throughout the department and blessed many lives. It was the celebration of a great man who went to heaven with his head held high as a proud son of His Father.

NOTES

Chapter 1

1. James Robison, conversation with author, September 13, 2021.

Chapter 2

1. Ken Harrison, "Excellence Isn't a Destination—It's an Identity, with Chad Hennings," January 14, 2021, in *On the Edge with Ken Harrison*, podcast, https://www.youtube.com/watch?v=BBZVxGMuxh8.

Chapter 3

1. Tim Dunn, conversation with author, September 10, 2021.
2. Randall Murphree, "What Are You Living For?" *AFA Journal*, July/August 2014, https://afajournal.org/past-issues/2014/july-august/what-are-you-living-for/.
3. Richard Cavendish, "Latimer and Ridley Burned at the Stake," *History Today*, October 10, 2005, https://www.historytoday.com/archive/months-past/latimer-and-ridley-burned-stake.

Chapter 4

1. James Robison, conversation with author, October 21, 2021.

Chapter 5

1. "Addison Bevere: We Are Saints," interview by James Robison, LIFE Today TV, streamed live on January 20, 2020, https://www.youtube.com/watch?v=ABiPaQICneE.

2. Ted Shimer, *The Freedom Fight: The New Drug and the Truths That Set Us Free* (Houston: High Bridge Books, 2020), 25.

3. Shimer, *Freedom Fight*, 24.

Chapter 6

1. Tim Dunn, conversation with author, September 10, 2021.

Chapter 7

1. George Whitefield, *The Works of the Reverend George Whitefield* (London: Edward and Charles Dilly, 1771), 1:385, https://www.google.com/books/edition/The_Works_of_the_Reverend_George_Whitefi/-l9XAAAAcAAJ?hl=en&gbpv=0. Spelling has been modernized for clarity.

2. There are two Greek words for "carnal": *sarkinos*, which means "immature," and *sarkikos*, which means "self-centered, immoral." Both are found in 1 Corinthians 3:1–3 (*sarkinos*, v. 1; *sarkikos*, v. 3).

3. Robert Mason, conversation with author, January 4, 2022.

4. Steven Pressfield, *Gates of Fire* (Australia: Doubleday, 1998).

Chapter 8

1. Greg Stier, conversation with author, August 3, 2021.

2. "Jesus the Stone Mason," *National Geographic*, YouTube video, 3:00, December 13, 2010, https://www.youtube.com/watch?v=wCp-428cvyE.

3. See Joseph Dillow, *Final Destiny: The Future Reign of the Servant Kings* (self-pub., 2012), ch. 54–57.

Chapter 9

1. Oswald Chambers, *My Utmost for His Highest* (New York: Dodd, Mead, & Co., 1935).

Chapter 10

1. Dillow, *Final Destiny*, 223.

2. Dillow, 848.
3. Dillow, 848.
4. Dillow, 1029.

Chapter 11

1. Winston Churchill, "Speech to Parliament, May 13, 1940," Mount Holyoke, accessed January 17, 2022, https://www .mtholyoke.edu/acad/intrel/speech/blood.htm.
2. Erwin Lutzer, *Your Eternal Reward: Triumph and Tears at the Judgment Seat of Christ* (Chicago: Moody Publishers, 2015), 143.
3. Klaus W. Larres, "When a Winner Becomes a Loser: Winston Churchill Was Kicked Out of Office in the British Election of 1945," The Conversation, July 27, 2020, https://theconversation .com/when-a-winner-becomes-a-loser-winston-churchill-was -kicked-out-of-office-in-the-british-election-of-1945-129746.

Chapter 12

1. Charles Spurgeon, "How to Become Fishers of Men," sermon from Metropolitan Tabernacle Pulpit, vol. 32, Spurgeon Center Digital Library, accessed January 17, 2022, https://www .spurgeon.org/resource-library/sermons/how-to-become -fishers-of-men/#flipbook/.

ACKNOWLEDGMENTS

I OWE A GREAT DEBT OF GRATITUDE TO ONE OF THE GREAT minds on the subject of life after death for Christians, Dr. Joseph (Jody) Dillow. Dr. Dillow has written an exhaustive and comprehensive work on the judgment seat of Christ and rewards and crowns called *Final Destiny* (it is the updated version of his book *Reign of the Future Servant Kings*). I leaned heavily both on his book as well as on many conversations with Jody where I grilled him with tough questions. If you wish to take a deep dive into these issues, I can't suggest Dillow's book more enthusiastically.

Heaven, a book by my good friend Randy Alcorn, was another great resource, as well as works by Erwin Lutzer (especially *Your Eternal Reward*), Andrew Murray, and G. K. Chesterton.

There is a long list of very special people who have contributed their wisdom to this work: the boards of Promise Keepers and WaterStone, especially Doug Kieswetter, John Mulder, Pastor Sam Rodriguez, Senator James Lankford, Pastor Steve Berger, Pastor Donald Burgs, Chad Hennings, Del DeWindt, Pastor A. R. Bernard, and Judge Vance Day.

ACKNOWLEDGMENTS

Of course, my biggest thanks go to my wife, Elliette, and our children, Ashton, Hunter, and Coleman. Elliette's relentless dedication to giving her all to build God's kingdom has been rewarded richly in this world by three adult children who reflect their mother's love of Christ. All three of our children never cease to amaze me in their dedication to our Lord. They are arrows in our quiver and great saints.

ABOUT THE AUTHOR

KEN HARRISON started his career as a Los Angeles police officer in the infamous 77th Division of South-Central Los Angeles, better known as Watts or Compton, where he received numerous commendations and awards. After leaving the LAPD in the 1990s, Ken went into business and built a small local company into one of the biggest of its kind in the United States.

In 2006, Ken sold his company to the second-largest commercial real estate firm in the world, continuing to run the US company and chairing the global operation. When the bond market collapsed in 2008, creating the biggest real estate recession in history, competing companies decreased their work forces or closed their doors. Instead, Ken's company tripled revenues and quadrupled profits.

Ken has spoken on diverse areas of leadership to tens of thousands of people throughout the world and appeared on television and radio shows, such as *Huckabee*, BlazeTV, Fox News, One America News Network (OAN), *Dr. James Dobson's Family Talk*, *Life Today TV with James & Betty Robison*, and

The 700 Club. He has served on multiple boards, including as chairman of Promise Keepers. Ken is the author of *Rise of the Servant Kings*, which explores what the Bible says about masculinity.

Ken has been married to his wife, Elliette, for thirty-one years and has three children, Ashton, Hunter, and Coleman. They live in Castle Rock, Colorado. Ken is currently CEO of WaterStone, a Christian foundation that gives away just over $2 million per week, and the volunteer chairman and CEO of Promise Keepers.